Leadership Theory and

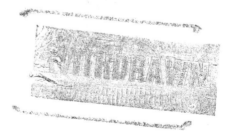

Christian Harrison

Leadership Theory and Research

A Critical Approach to New and Existing Paradigms

Christian Harrison
School of Business and Enterprise
University of the West of Scotland
Hamilton, UK

ISBN 978-3-319-68671-4   ISBN 978-3-319-68672-1   (eBook)
https://doi.org/10.1007/978-3-319-68672-1

Library of Congress Control Number: 2017955201

Cover illustration: Cover pattern © Harvey Loake

Printed on acid-free paper

This Palgrave Macmillan imprint is published by Springer Nature
The registered company is Springer International Publishing AG
The registered company address is: Gewerbestrasse 11, 6330 Cham, Switzerland

First and foremost, I will like to express my gratitude to God for giving me the grace and strength to complete this book. Without God it would not have been possible.
This book is dedicated to my wife, Anuoluwapo Laura Harrison, whose love and patience has inspired me. Thank you for being there for me through thick and thin and believing in me. To my son and daughter, Christian Harrison, Jr and Lily Harrison, I hope one day you will both read this book and be inspired. You motivate me every day, and this work is dedicated to you and your mum.

Foreword

It is with great pleasure that we introduce Christian Harrison's book, *Leadership Theory and Research: A Critical Approach to New and Existing Paradigms*. It is a terrific achievement and fills a much-needed gap in terms of providing educators and students with a clear and comprehensive introduction to the topic of leadership. Concise and accessible, it provides also a depth of explanation of some of the main theories relating to leadership and change, and it offers a wealth of relevant references that are invaluable for those seeking to navigate the field.

A considerable strength of the work is its emphasis on a nuanced conceptualisation of leadership. This puts into context the limitations of fixed notions of human development that have influenced a range of leadership theories and even some current work-based interventions. In a concise retrospective of the development of the discipline, the book presents a very useful account of older, more recent and current theories of leadership, bringing the reader up to date with contemporary thought. A further strength of the book is the insight the author brings to these overviews, with relevant critique where the findings across a range of empirical studies are inconclusive. Thus, *Leadership Theory and Research* is a very useful introduction to each of the main theories that have been applied to leadership over the last century or so, but does not present these unchallenged. For the reader, this introduces the idea that critical engagement with literature is important in terms of development of skills and abilities as a scholar, and educators will find this a useful resource for the development of these types of skills.

At a more specific level, there are two particular areas where *Leadership Theory and Research* really stands out. First, there is a contribution specifically to the leadership discourse in entrepreneurial settings. The relevance and specificities of leadership for entrepreneurs are examined and critiqued, and as a result, this book is useful as an introductory text to those studying entrepreneurship as well as other management and leadership subjects. The second particular strength is the identification of, and subsequent contribution to, an ongoing gap in leadership studies. In *Leadership Theory and Research*, the dearth of studies of leadership outside the contexts of the dominant Western cultures is highlighted. As Dr. Harrison points out though, leadership happens everywhere and always has done. Consequently—and somewhat uniquely—the text draws on a number of studies in the global east and south. This is a considerable strength of the work; the inclusion of evidence and consideration of leadership underpinned by alternative (to Western) cultural and structural conditions are rarely included in textbooks, and its inclusion here broadens our perspective beyond assuming the primacy of Western thought. More broadly, the contribution in *Leadership Theory and Research* underlines the value of inclusive thinking in leadership and, by drawing attention to the domination of the field by scholars in the developed world, allows readers to critically engage with scholarship on leadership.

The structure of the book is clear, with effective signposting in introductions and summaries at the start and end of each chapter. Readers will value the author's concise writing style which makes the presentation of complex aspects of leadership highly accessible. New scholars to the field or those seeking an introduction to key ideas will find the work an enjoyable and rewarding read. Dr. Harrison's skill of getting to the point of a particular theory will be especially valuable to the busy reader who will find useful insights on every page.

As educators in higher education, we would have no hesitation using *Leadership Theory and Research* in classes. As an introductory text, it provides a comprehensive account of the theories of leadership and draws clearly from many sources of research on the topic. There are several textbooks on leadership in the market, but this one really fills a gap in terms of its simplicity and accessibility for those new to the subject. Beyond this, *Leadership Theory and Research* is a useful resource for developing skills in critical engagement with research and theory. From this perspective, there is utility also for the more advanced student of leadership. Its specific inclusion of leadership for entrepreneurship is an attractive addition to the text. Finally, the inclusion of analysis of studies of leadership in contexts that represent experiences alternative to those in the Western, developed world provides a much-needed contribution to the field.

We both thoroughly enjoyed reading this book—and we both have come away from it with ideas about how we will teach leadership as a conceptualisation and in terms of skills development going forward. For us at least, *Leadership Theory and Research* will be a welcome addition to our resources for the learning and teaching of leadership, and we commend this book to you.

Dr. Irene Malcolm
Learning & Teaching Co-ordinator
Heriot-Watt University
Currie, UK

Professor Laura Galloway
Edinburgh Business School
Edinburgh, UK

Preface

Leadership is a phenomenon observed in all organised human groups. However, research has shown that it is one of the least understood phenomena on earth. The number of published research studies in the field of leadership is vast and spans several decades. Nevertheless, despite such a large body of scholarship, leadership still remains an elusive concept.

This book provides a comprehensive literature review on leadership. The aim is to provide a critical insight into leadership research. Emerging paradigms and theories of new approaches to leadership are identified and addressed. Though there have been books that examined leadership theories and approaches, these writers do not take a critical view of the different leadership perspectives. In this age of globalisation and increased competition, there is a need for individuals to use the most effective leadership approach. This book has established that leadership is an underdeveloped phenomenon, for which no unified theory currently exists. Previous leadership books have traditionally focused narrowly on a limited set of elements by highlighting the leader while overlooking relevant elements of leadership. This book takes a holistic view of the phenomenon.

This book will enable students (undergraduate and postgraduate), scholars, practitioners, policymakers and other relevant stakeholders to learn more about the concept of leadership. They will be able to display critical awareness of current developments in both the theory and practice of leadership and its importance in modern organisations. This critical reflection will be instrumental in meeting the leadership development needs of twenty-first century graduates as well as identifying potential sources of development.

Most books on leadership tend to be monographs which are quite lengthy and monotonous. Such monographs do not encourage readers especially students and practitioners. Readers are looking for a book that is easy to read and provides a detailed summary of the approaches to leadership. This book offers the solution and a good snap shot on leadership. The book is not only for scholars but also for practitioners, students (undergraduate and postgraduate) and policymakers.

Benefits of the Book

- The reader will be able to explain the concept of leadership.
- The reader will be able to assess the different theories of leadership and its importance in modern organisations.
- The reader will be able to critically reflect on leadership development needs of twenty-first century graduates and identify potential sources of development.

Christian Harrison
School of Business and Enterprise
University of the West of Scotland
Hamilton, UK

Acknowledgements

Indeed, no list of acknowledgments can be complete. So many people have assisted in this project. Among the many people, I will like to thank Prof. Laura Galloway and Prof. Rob Smith for persuading me to write this book in the first place. This is one of the best decisions I have made. I am eternally grateful. I would also like to give special thanks to Dr. Stuart Paul (Ph.D. Supervisor), who encouraged my research in leadership and was able to spark my passion and interest in this field. Also, thanks go to Dr. Kevin Burnard who was an important part of my supervisory team and the great faculty at the University of the West of Scotland that mentored me during my days in the Ph.D. programme.

My colleagues over the years from the University of the West of Scotland and Birmingham City University cannot go without mention. Your support and ideas made this project possible and I owe you all my biggest thanks. I will also like to give special acknowledgements to all my students (undergraduate, postgraduate taught and Ph.D.). You have been a source of inspiration in writing this book.

It would be a remiss not to mention the support of my family. First, my mother, Stella Harrison, for her unconditional love and support during the early years of my life, and to date, you have been a true believer in me. My brothers, Charles and George, for always challenging and believing in my abilities and my uncles, aunties, mother-in-law, brother-in-law, sisters-in-law and friends, without whom, this would not have been possible.

Finally, I will like to thank the people of Palgrave Macmillan who helped make this project possible. Special thanks go to Liz Barlow and Lucy Kidwell. They provided tremendous support through the writing and production phase of the book.

Contents

1 Introduction   1
  Introduction   2
  The Definitions of Leadership   2
  Leadership and Management   3
  Case Study 1.1   9
    Manager or Leader?   9
  Summary   10
  References   11

2 Leadership Research and Theory   15
  Introduction   16
  Great Man Theory   17
  Trait Theory   19
  Skill Theory   21
  Case Study 2.1   21
    Skill Perspective—Apollo 13   21
  Behavioural Theory   23
  Case Study 2.2   26
    Leadership Style   26

Contingency Theory   27
Summary   29
References   29

3   **Emerging Paradigms**   33
Introduction   34
Implicit Leadership Theories   34
Leader–Member Exchange Theory   35
Case Study 3.1   36
   Leader–Member Exchange   36
Servant Leadership Theory   37
Case Study 3.2   40
   Servant Leadership   40
Charismatic Leadership Theory   41
Case Study 3.3   43
   Charismatic Leadership   43
Transactional Leadership Theory   45
Case Study 3.4   45
   Transactional Leadership   45
Transformational Leadership Theory   47
Case Study 3.5   49
   Transformational Leadership   49
Distributed Leadership Theory   51
Case Study 3.6   52
   Distributed Leadership   52
Authentic Leadership Theory   53
Case Study 3.7   55
   Authentic Leadership   55
Entrepreneurial Leadership Theory   57
   Conceptions of Entrepreneurial Leadership   58
   A Convergence of Entrepreneurship and Leadership   58
   Psychological and Behavioural Profile of Entrepreneurial
   Leaders   59
   Context of Entrepreneurial Leadership   60
   Theoretical Approach to Entrepreneurial Leadership   61

Entrepreneurial Leadership Compared with Other Forms
of Leadership   62
Entrepreneurial Leadership and Values   62
Entrepreneurial Leadership Education   62
Entrepreneurial Leadership and Venture Performance   63
Case Study 3.8   63
Entrepreneurial Leadership   63
Summary   65
References   67

4 Conclusion   79
Introduction   80
Technical Skills   80
Human Skills   81
Conceptual Skills   82
Other Leadership Skills   84
Business Skills   84
Conceptual Skills   85
Interpersonal Skills   88
Entrepreneurial Skills   91
Leadership Skills Development   93
Mentoring   93
Leadership Training Programmes   94
Personal Growth Activities   95
Summary   95
References   96

Index   103

List of Tables

Table 1.1 Definitions of leadership   4

Table 3.1 Strengths and weaknesses of some of the theories
           of leadership   66

1

Introduction

Abstract This chapter provides a comprehensive literature review on leadership. The aim is to provide a critical insight into leadership research. This chapter discusses the varying conceptions of leadership. Scholars argue that a universally acceptable definition for leadership is practically impossible and will hinder creative ways of thinking. Some of the different ways in which leadership has been defined over the past 70 years with reference to conceptual underpinning are provided in this chapter. The distinction between leadership and management is often made in the literature. However, in the world today, a question remains unanswered which is: Is leadership now increasingly needed by all managers? This chapter examines the similarities and differences between leadership and management. The functions and activities of management and leadership are discussed.

Keywords Leadership conceptions · Definitions of leadership
Leadership · Management · Roles of leaders · Roles of managers

Introduction

The number of published research studies in the field of leadership is vast and spans several decades. However, despite such a large body of scholarship, leadership still remains an elusive concept. Despite considerable investment in research by both governments and organisations, knowledge gaps about leadership still exist due to a lack of comprehensive information studies of the field (Leitch et al. 2009).

This chapter provides a comprehensive literature review on leadership. The aim is to provide a critical insight into leadership research. This chapter will discuss the varying conceptions of leadership. Scholars argue that a universally acceptable definition for leadership is practically impossible and will hinder new ideas and creative ways of thinking. Some of the different ways in which leadership has been defined over the past 70 years with reference to conceptual underpinning are provided in this chapter.

The distinction between leadership and management is often made in the literature. However in the world today, a question remains unanswered which is: Is leadership now increasingly needed by all managers? This chapter will examine the similarities and differences between leadership and management. The functions and activities of management and leadership are discussed.

The Definitions of Leadership

To date, there is no precise definition of the term leadership. Stogdill (1974, p. 259) argued that '...there are almost as many different definitions of leadership as there are people who have attempted to define the concept'. This is evident, given the large volume of publications and studies relating to the domain of leadership. Upon entering the search string 'lead*' into Web of Science, 2,122,285 publications were listed, and on Springer Link, 4,333,478 publications in form of journals and books were identified as being relevant to the topic (17th January 2017). Researchers have proposed varying concepts of leadership and have investigated it by using different phenomena that suited them (Yukl 2010). This is not surprising because, although leadership is a universal phenomenon (Bass and Bass 2009), it remains complex. Alvesson and Sveningsson (2003) argue that a universally acceptable definition for leadership is practically impossible and will hinder new ideas and creative ways of thinking. Some of the different ways in which leadership has been defined over the past 70 years, with reference to conceptual underpinning, are listed in Table 1.1.

The definitions listed in the table demonstrate how the perception of leadership has evolved from it being viewed as an ability or behaviour to being viewed as a process of influence. The section below examines the similarities and differences between leadership and management.

Leadership and Management

Leadership and Management have been used interchangeably in the literature and rightly so. In fact, they are synonymous in various ways since they both involve working with people and meeting set goals (Northouse 2010). However, this view is not shared by all scholars in the domain of leadership and management. Many authors have argued that there is a difference between leadership and management (Bennis and Nanus 1985; Kotter 1990; Rost 1993; Zaleznik 1977). The major bone of contention has been the definition and functions of both leaders and managers.

Management has been defined as the 'attainment of organisational goals in an effective and efficient manner through planning, organising, leading and controlling organisational resources' (Daft et al. 2010, p. 7). According to Robbins (2005), it involves the use of authority inherent in a designated formal rank to obtain compliance from members of an organisation. It encompasses getting things done through other people in order to achieve stated objectives (Mullins 1996). The focus of the definitions provided by these scholars shows that the intent of management is to meet organisational goals in an efficient and effective manner. Conversely, leadership which has been defined in the previous section is

Table 1.1 Definitions of leadership

Author	Definition	Concept
Hemphill (1949)	The behaviour of an individual while he is involved in directing group activities	Behaviour
Stogdill (1950)	'Leadership may be considered as the process (act) of influencing the activities of an organized group in its efforts toward goal setting and goal achievement'	Process
Bennis (1959)	Leadership is 'the process by which an agent induces a subordinate to behave in a desired manner'	Process
Katz and Kahn (1978)	Leadership is 'the influential increment over and above mechanical compliance with the routine directives of the organisation'	Behavioural process
Smircich and Morgan (1982)	'Leadership is realised in the process whereby one or more individuals succeeds in attempting to frame and define the reality of other.' 'It involves a complicity or process of negotiation through which certain individuals implicitly or explicitly surrender their power to define the nature of their experience to others'	Process
Richards and Engle (1986)	'Leadership is about articulating visions, embodying values, and creating the environment within which things can be accomplished'	Behaviour

(continued)

Table 1.1 (continued)

Author	Definition	Concept
Gardner (1990)	Leadership is 'the process of persuasion or example by which an individual (or leadership team) induces a group to pursue objectives held by the leader or shared by the leader and his or her follower'	Process
Jacobs and Jaques (1990)	'Leadership is a process of giving purpose (meaningful direction) to collective effort, and causing willing effort to be expended to achieve purpose'	Process
Kotter (1990)	Leadership 'refers to a process that helps direct and mobilize people and/or their ideas...'	Process
Drath and Palus (1994)	'Leadership is the process of making sense of what people are doing together so that people will understand and be committed'	Process
Clark and Clark (1996)	'Leadership is an activity or set of activities, observable to others, that occurs in a group, organization, or institution, and which involves a leader and followers who willingly subscribe to common purposes and work together to achieve them'	Process
Barnard (1997)	Leadership 'refers to the quality of the behaviour of individuals guiding other people or their activities in organized efforts'	Behaviour

(continued)

Table 1.1 (continued)

Author	Definition	Concept
Stogdill (1997)	Leadership is 'the process of influencing the activities of an organised group in its efforts towards goal-setting and goal achievement'	Process
Robbins (1998)	Leadership is 'the ability to influence a group toward the achievement of goals'	Ability
Barker (2001)	Leadership is 'a process of transformative change where the ethics of individuals are integrated into the mores of a community as a means of evolutionary social development'	Process
Lussier and Achua (2001)	'Leadership is the influencing process of leaders and followers to achieve organizational objectives through change'	Process
Northouse (2010)	'Leadership is a process whereby an individual influences a group of individuals to achieve a common goal'	Process
Yukl (2010)	'Leadership is the process of influencing others to understand and agree about what needs to be done and how to do it, and the process of facilitating individual and collective efforts to accomplish shared objectives'	Process

more complex and deals with other variables such as influence, motivation, change and not just meeting the organisational objectives.

The function of management and leadership is also a source of controversy among scholars. Kotter (1990) argues that leaders cope with change while managers deal with complexity. For Kotter, leaders develop a vision and strategies for achieving the vision while managers are involved in planning and budgeting. Leaders and managers are totally different in their attitude towards goals and conception of work (Zaleznik 1977). This is not surprising since the functions of management have long been established in the literature. Fayol (1916) first identified the functions of management as planning, organising, staffing and controlling. These functions have been supported and modified by other scholars such as Kotter (1990) to include budgeting and problem-solving.

Some scholars have used the terminology 'roles'. Mintzberg (1973) proposed ten managerial roles from his study on executives which are provided below.

Information Processing Roles

- Disseminator
- Monitor
- Spokesperson

Interpersonal Roles

- Figurehead
- Leader
- Liaison

Decision-Making Roles

- Disturbance handler
- Entrepreneur
- Negotiator
- Resource allocator

Conversely, in leadership, the key activities or roles are quite distinct. Kotter (1990) describes the key leadership activities as setting a direction, aligning people in that direction, motivating and inspiring. It involves developing a mutual purpose by both the leaders and followers as well as working together to create change (Rost 1993).

Despite the constant debate and inability to reach a consensus by both fields of management and leadership, it is arguable that not everyone who is a manager will necessarily be a leader and vice versa. To some extent, different characteristics, skills, focus and style are required. Managers have to know how to plan, budget, organise staff as well as control and solve problems in an effective and efficient manner. Their focus is on physical resources usually materials and people, and as Bennis and Nanus (1985, p. 21) point out, they 'do things right'. For leaders, their role is to set the direction and to ensure that the required expertise, resources and motivation is present. Their focus is on emotional resources; hence, they ought to show empathy, build trust, respect and enthusiasm and of course still referring to Bennis and Nanus (1985, p. 21) they 'do the right things'.

Despite the differences, it is quite clear that both management and leadership are useful in today's world. If there is no strong leadership, people would not be motivated. If there is no strong management, the established organisational goals may not be achieved. So what then is the solution? We need both competent managers and skilled leaders. Sayles (1993) argues that leadership is important in management and that organisations cannot function effectively without middle managers who can exercise leadership. Scholars such as Daft et al. (2010), Mintzberg (1973) and Mullins (1996) propose that leadership is an activity or role that managers ought to be involved. They are both interlinked and cannot be viewed independently. Managers will need to learn how to lead while leaders have to learn how to manage. With a more educated and diverse work force who are not so concerned about pay, motivation and other soft elements have become very important. The work place has increasingly become insecure in the twenty-first century; hence, using emotional support to counter resistance and promote a more conducive working environment is paramount.

Case Study 1.1

Manager or Leader?

Jeffrey Preston 'Jeff' Bezos is an American technology entrepreneur who has played a key role in the growth of e-commerce as the founder and CEO of Amazon.com, the online merchant of books and later of a wide variety of products. Under his leadership, Amazon.com became the largest retailer on the World Wide Web.

In 2012, Amazon reached an interesting mile stone. This retailing giant known for books and media products now has tens of millions of products in stock. Interestingly, most of these products are non-media goods. Amazon has been officially transformed from an online book retailer to a worldwide product merchant that can meet the needs of the diverse population.

Jeff Bezos is one of the richest men in the world with a net worth of about $72.8 billion (Forbes 2017). However, his success is largely due to his mantra 'The customer is always right'. In an era, where the focus is on team working and making the employees happy, Bezos has proven the potency of another model; 'coddling his 164 million customers, not his 56,000 employees' (Forbes 2012a).

His managers find him formidable. He is referred to as the 'empty chair'. This is because Bezos periodically during meetings leaves one seat empty at a conference table and tells his staff to assume that a customer is occupying that seat and is the most important person in the room. This seems comical but Bezos takes it seriously as confirmed by his managers. He is also strict about what the customers do not want. There is so much focus on reducing delays, defects and out of stock products. Even the tiniest delay in loading a web page is frowned at and not acceptable. Indeed, all the people that know him attest that he has an obsession for the customer.

There is so much focus on pragmatism, and it has shaped his decision-making. The three big ideas of Amazon are long-term thinking, customer obsession and a willingness to invent (Fortune 2012). Bezos is not afraid of failure and is willing to take risks. For him, 'if you want to be inventive, you have to be willing to fail' (Forbes 2012b). This is reflected early in the company when they hired a lot of editors to write book and music reviews and then decided to use customer critiques instead. This affected the auctions negatively. Bezos regards this as a learning curve. The culture of Amazon is friendly but intense. It is termed the 'culture of metrics' (Forbes 2012a, b) with little time for socialisation. This is not strange because of his attention to detail. He is widely known for being meticulous and some might even argue that he has the tendency to micromanage.

With the huge success of Amazon, it is hard to believe that it all started in a garage in Seattle Water front by a teenager who had earlier wanted to be an astronaut and was also the high school valedictorian as well as a National Merit Scholar. The success story of Amazon has not ended and many believe that with Bezos still at the helm of affairs, this may just be the beginning.

Questions

- Is Bezos a manager or a leader or both?
- Is Bezos the right person for Amazon during the times ahead, or does the company now require more of a 'manager' than a 'leader'?

Summary

In this chapter, the concept of leadership and its different definitions were examined. Leadership is intuitively appealing; hence, numerous definitions have been proposed by scholars. However, despite such a large body of scholarship, leadership still remains an elusive concept.

Leadership and Management is a source of debate among scholars. These concepts tend to overlap. They are similar as well as different. The activities and roles that define both concepts are important, especially in today's world. Traditionally, management is viewed through the lens of planning, organising, controlling and coordinating while leadership involves exerting influence. However, these boundaries are getting more obscure in the twenty-first century. It has become more difficult to view them independently. Managers will need to learn how to lead while leaders have to learn how to manage.

References

Alvesson, M., & Sveningsson, S. (2003). The great disappearing act: Difficulties in doing "leadership". *The Leadership Quarterly, 14*(3), 359–381.

Barker, R. A. (2001). The nature of leadership. *Human Relations, 54*(4), 469–494.

Barnard, C. (1997). The nature of leadership. In K. Grint (Ed.), *Leadership, classical, contemporary, and critical approaches.* Oxford University Press; Original publication Organization and Management, Cambridge, Massachusetts: Harvard University Press, 1948.

Bass, B. M., & Bass, R. (2009). *The bass handbook of leadership: Theory, research, and managerial applications* (4th ed.). New York: Free Press.

Bennis, W. G. (1959). Leadership theory and administrative behavior: The problem of authority. *Administrative Science Quarterly, 4*(1), 259–301.

Bennis, W. G., & Nanus, B. (1985). *Leaders: The strategies for taking charge.* New York: Harper & Row.

Clark, K. E., & Clark, M. B. (1996). *Choosing to lead.* Greensboro, North Carolina: Center for Creative Leadership.

Daft, R. L., Kendrick, M., & Vershinina, N. (2010). *Management.* Singapore: South Western Cengage Learning.

Drath, W. H., & Palus, C. J. (1994). *Making common sense: Leadership as meaning-making in a community of practice.* Greensboro, North Carolina: Center for Creative Leadership.

Fayol, H. (1916). *General and industrial management.* London: Pittman Publishing.

Forbes. (2012a). Inside Amazon's idea machine: How Bezos decodes customers. https://www.forbes.com/sites/georgeanders/2012/04/04/inside-amazon/#6fac29e96199. Accessed May 22, 2017.

Forbes. (2012b). Jeff Bezos's top 10 leadership lessons. https://www.forbes.com/sites/georgeanders/2012/04/04/bezos-tips/#3870d822fce4. Accessed May 22, 2017.

Forbes. (2017). Forbes 2017 billionaires list: Meet the richest people on the planet. https://www.forbes.com/sites/kerryadolan/2017/03/20/forbes-2017-billionaires-list-meet-the-richest-people-on-the-planet/#357ff1a262ff. Accessed May 22, 2017.

Fortune. (2012). Amazon's Jeff Bezos: The ultimate disrupter. http://fortune. com/2012/11/16/amazons-jeff-bezos-the-ultimate-disrupter/. Accessed May 22, 2017.

Gardner, J. W. (1990). *On leadership*. New York: Free Press.

Hemphill, J. K. (1949). *Situational factors in leadership*. Columbus: Ohio State University.

Jacobs, T. O., & Jaques, E. (1990). Military executive leadership. In K. E. Clark & M. B. Clark (Eds.), *Measures of leadership* (pp. 281–295). West Orange, New Jersey: Leadership Library of America.

Katz, D., & Kahn, R. L. (1978). *The social psychology of organizations* (2nd ed.). New York: Wiley.

Kotter, J. P. (1990). *A force for change: How leadership differs from management*. New York: Free Press.

Leitch, C. M., McMullan, C., & Harrison, R. T. (2009). Leadership development in SMEs: An action learning approach. *Action Learning: Research and Practice, 6*(3), 243–263.

Lussier, R. N., & Achua, C. F. (2001). *Leadership: Theory, application & skill development*. Ohio: South Western College Publishing, Thomson learning.

Mintzberg, H. (1973). *The Nature of managerial work*. New York: Harper and Row.

Mullins, L. J. (1996). *Management and organizational behavior* (4th ed.). London: Pittman Publishing.

Northouse, P. G. (2010). *Leadership: Theory and practice* (5th ed.). California: Sage.

Richards, D., & Engle, S. (1986). After the vision: suggestions to corporate visionaries and vision champions. In J. D. Adams (Ed.), *Transforming leadership* (pp. 199–215). Alexandria, Virginia: Miles River Press.

Robbins, S. (1998). *Organizational behavior: Concepts, controversies, applications*. Upper Saddle River: Prentice Hall International.

Robbins, S. P. (2005). *Organizational behavior* (11th ed.). Upper Saddle River, New Jersey: Prentice-Hall.

Rost, J. C. (1993). *Leadership for the Twenty-First Century*. New York: Praeger.

Sayles, L. R. (1993). *The Working Leader*. New York: Free Press.

Smircich, L., & Morgan, G. (1982). Leadership: The management of meaning. *Journal of Applied Behavioral Science, 18*(3), 257–273.

Stogdill, R. M. (1950). Leadership, membership and organization. *Psychological Bulletin, 47*(1), 1–14.

Stogdill, R. M. (1974). *Handbook of Leadership*. New York: Free Press.

Stogdill. R. M. (1997). Leadership, Membership, and Organization. In K. Grint (Ed.), *Leadership, classical, contemporary, and critical approaches* (pp. 112–124), Oxford University Press; Original publication Psychological Bulletin, 47, 1950: 1–14.

Yukl, G. (2010). Leadership in organisations (7th ed). Upper Saddle River, New Jersey: Pearson Education Limited.

Zaleznik, A. (1977). Managers and leaders: Are they different? *Harvard Business Review, 55*(3), 67–78.

2

Leadership Research and Theory

Abstract Leadership theories are plagued by the absence of a definitional consensus among scholars. Many theories have emerged about leadership over the years. This chapter examines and evaluates the different early theories of leadership. The Great Man theory focuses on heroic individuals, implying that only a selected few can achieve greatness. The trait theory conceptualises leadership on the universality of some given attributes. The skill theory focuses on the abilities of a leader. Behavioural theory views leaders based on their actions and behaviour, while the contingency theory concerns the context of leadership. The shortcomings and limitations of these different theories, which have led to newer approaches to leadership, are also examined. Case studies are available to assess the reader's understanding of the relevant approaches in this chapter.

Keywords Leadership theories · Great Man theory · Trait theory Behavioural theory · Skill theory · Contingency theory

© The Author(s) 2018
C. Harrison, *Leadership Theory and Research*,
https://doi.org/10.1007/978-3-319-68672-1_2

Introduction

Leadership theories are plagued by the absence of a definitional consensus among scholars. Many theories have emerged about leadership over the years, and it might even be said that there are as many theories of leadership as there are leaders (Gill 2011). According to House and Aditya (1997, pp. 409–410),

> Almost all of the prevailing theories of leadership, and about 98% of the empirical evidence at hand, are rather distinctly American in character: individualistic rather than collectivistic, stressing follower responsibilities rather than rights, assuming hedonism rather than commitment to duty or altruistic motivation, assuming centrality of work and democratic value orientation, and emphasizing assumptions of rationality rather than asceticism, religion, or superstition.

This suggests that leadership research over time has developed a bias towards the outlooks of the developed world; hence, more research is required, especially from a developing economy perspective, to better understand this phenomenon.

Many approaches to leadership have emerged over the years. The main theories which can be identified are the Great Man, trait, skill, behaviour, contingency, implicit leadership, leader–member exchange, servant, charismatic, transactional, transformational, distributed, authentic and entrepreneurial leadership. Of these theories, entrepreneurial leadership is the least developed in terms of research and theory (Dinh et al. 2014). The timeline during which these leadership theories[1] emerged is illustrated in Fig. 2.1:

In this chapter, a critical overview of the early theories (i.e. Great Man, trait, skill, behaviour and contingency) is therefore presented.

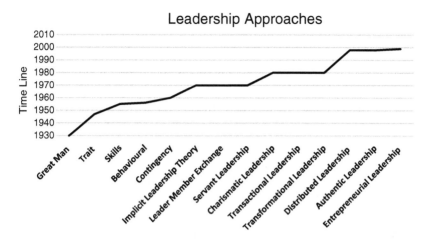

Fig. 2.1 Timeline showing the approaches to leadership

Great Man Theory

The Great Man theory of leadership can be traced to the nineteenth century and before. One of the major proponents of this theory was Carlyle in 1866, whose '…fascination with great men of history effectively reduced the role of mere mortals to extras' (Grint 2011, p. 8). Successful leaders who had shown greatness were examined; hence, the theories were called 'Great Man theories'. The lives and achievements of political leaders such as Napoleon Bonaparte, Indira Gandhi, Martin Luther King and others have been studied to explain the difference between people who are leaders and those who are non-leaders or followers. A fundamental notion of the Great Man theory is that people are born with traits that make them natural leaders, and only great individuals possess such traits. As stated by Bass and Bass (2009, p. 49), 'Without Moses, according to these theorists, the Jews would have remained in Egypt; without Winston Churchill, the British would have given up in 1940; without Bill Gates, there would have been no firm like Microsoft'. However, this theory is based on fascination with great men of history and has been criticised for its failure to explore the role of leadership in ensuring business and organisational coherence (Grint 2011).

In addition, this theory presents a gender bias as is seen in its name Great Man theory. This theory holds that history is attributed to men and great men actually change the shape and direction of history (Van Wart 2003). Leadership is irredeemably masculine, and the Great Man is indeed a man (Grint 2011; Spector 2016). Its basic premise is built on the fact that leadership is biologically determined, behaviourally demonstrated and innate to the male gender (Appelbaum et al. 2003). As a result, effective leadership can only be demonstrated by males. Surprisingly, during the period that the Great Man theory was proposed, there were notable female personalities who had shaped history but were overlooked. Typical examples such as Queen Elizabeth and Joan of Arc were heroes in their own rights. By ignoring gender, the scholars in this field created many blanks in theoretical and research designs (Denmark 1993). The exclusion of women in these studies may have been due to the limited number of women in that era that occupied leadership positions. However, times have changed and we now have more women in seats of power and are focal points in many businesses.

There has now been a plethora of studies that have focused on females in positions of authority. Successful female leaders such as Emma Walmsley of Glaxo SmithKline, Sheryl Sandberg of Facebook, Alison Brittain of Whitbread group, Carolyn McCall of EasyJet, Moya Green of Royal Mail, Veronique Laury of King Fisher, Alison Cooper of Imperial Tobacco and Liv Garfield of Seven Trent have formed the bulk of these studies. Studies have also shown that not only are men and women similar, women may be equally effective leaders (Kolb 1999; Shimanoff and Jenkins 1991). Nevertheless, despite studies such as Powell and Graves (2003) and Oakley (2000) that have shown that innate abilities of male and female managers are similar, stereotypes still persist that women are less capable and effective leaders than men (Appelbaum et al. 2003).

The Great Man theory, despite its lack of scientific rigour and veracity, remains relevant. In the world of business, the search for a hero to save failing companies still has a universal appeal (Spector 2016), and occasionally, this saviour is a woman.

Trait Theory

The Great Man theory, which attributed innate qualities to special peo-ple, resulted in research into leadership that focused on the personal-ity characteristics of the leader (Wright 1996). Researchers and scholars sought to determine the specific traits that differentiated leaders from followers (Bass 1990).

This theory led to an accumulation of a long list of traits. As stated by Wright (1996, p. 34), 'The problem was not the fact that the research failed to find any relationship between personality and leadership, but that relationships found were inconsistent'. One of the most influential studies on traits was carried out by Stogdill (1948), which changed the course of this approach. In his study, he analysed 124 trait studies con-ducted between 1904 and 1947 and identified eight traits that differen-tiate a leader from a non-leader. These are as follows:

- Intelligence
- Alertness to the needs of others
- Insight
- Initiative
- Responsibility
- Persistence in dealing with problems
- Self-confidence
- Sociability

Stogdill proposed that the making of a successful leader is not deter-mined by some particular traits but, rather, the traits possessed must be relevant to the situation in which a leader finds him or herself. Therefore, a successful leader in a particular situation might be inef-fective in another. The results of Stogdill's work led many scholars to re-examine their approach in the search for universal traits. House and Aditya (1997, p. 410) point out that, 'It should be noted, however, that the most influential author to address this issue (Stogdill 1948) did not call for an abandonment of the study of traits, but rather for an inter-actional approach in which traits would be considered as interacting with situational demands facing leaders'. Mann (1959) went a stage further by examining more than 1400 findings regarding personality and leadership. He drew up a list of traits such as intelligence, masculinity, adjustment, extraversion, conservatism and dominance, all of which had been considered as important, but then pointed out that there were inconsistencies in results of studies showing relationships between leadership and some of the traits such as dominance, extraversion and intelligence.

Many more scholars undertook further studies into traits, and endless lists of traits emerged. Traits such as dominance, high energy, achievement orientation, the need for power, a moderately low need for affiliation, internal locus of control, integrity, flexibility, self-confidence, stability, intelligence, sensitivity to others and narcissism have been deemed as being important to leadership, according to researchers (Bass and Bass 2009; Lord et al. 1986; Lussier and Achua 2001; McClelland 1965, 1975, 1985; Northouse 2010; Yukl 2010). Despite this long list of personality traits, the picture of personal qualities of leadership is still not complete (Gill 2011). There is no evidence to prove that leaders who possess all the identified traits mentioned in prior studies will be effective. In addition, how realistic is it for a leader to possess all traits that have been associated with effective leadership? House and Aditya (1997, p. 410) suggest that, 'One of the problems with early trait research was there was little empirically substantiated personality theory to guide the search for leadership'. The broad range of traits has made them susceptible to various subjective interpretations, and the origin of these lists is not based on strong empirical research. Moreover, the trait approach does not effectively justify the role of leadership in entrepreneurial settings. However, in recent years, the trait approach has re-emerged in the form of charismatic and transformational leadership (that will be discussed later in this book). Despite the aforementioned criticisms, the trait theory still remains a popular theory of leadership due to its intuitive appeal and its use of benchmarks for identifying effective leaders (Northouse 2010).

Skill Theory

Although leadership studies began with the concept of the 'Great Man', in which a leader is seen as born and not made, Katz (1955) proposed a shift from a focus on personality traits to an emphasis on skills and abilities of individuals that can be learned and developed (Northouse 2010). Therefore, the major difference between the trait approach and the skill approach was that, unlike the traits (which were said to be innate and cannot be learned), skills or competencies could be developed. Katz (1955) put forward three skills which he argued were essential to being an effective administrator—technical, human and conceptual skills.

More recently, Mumford et al. (2000a) advanced three key leadership competencies, which are problem-solving, social judgement and knowledge skills. The skill approach, unlike the trait approach, provides a broader perspective on leadership. It shifts the focus on leadership being just for a selected few but to a new mindset that everybody can be a leader if they so desire and are ready to acquire the necessary skills and competencies. But although it claims to be quite different from the trait perspective, the major component of Mumford et al.'s (2000a) research on leadership skills was individual attributes which are trait-like; hence, the skill-based approach is still trait driven (Northouse 2010). In addition, most of the skills originated from research in the army neglecting the entrepreneurial context (Mumford et al. 2000a, b). The skill perspective is discussed in more detail in Chap. 4.

Case Study 2.1

Skill Perspective—Apollo 13

Apollo 13 was the third intended mission in the American space programme to land on the Moon. On 11 April 1970, astronauts Jim Lovell, Fred Haise and Jack Swigert blasted-off towards the moon. After almost three days of smooth operations, an oxygen tank on board the craft blew up, sending the crews on board and at National Aeronautics and Space Administration's (NASA) Houston-based command centre into overdrive to get the spacecraft back to earth with its inhabitants alive. The explosion triggered a series of dilemmas, one following another, that lasted several more days. They quickly lose oxygen, run out of power and got exposed to dangerously high amounts of carbon dioxide. Intensifying the situation is the fact that these mishaps caught the scientists and technicians at Mission Control by surprise, and they are not sure how to remedy the situation.

Considerable ingenuity under extreme pressure was required from the crew, flight controllers and support personnel for the safe return. However, many people agree that the leadership of Gene Kranz, the NASA flight director who served during the Apollo 13 crisis, was invaluable in ensuring that the crew were able to return to earth safely.

A movie (Grazer and Howard 1995) has been made to portray what happened in space and some quotes found below show some of the leadership displayed by Gene Kranz while in crisis:

Work the problem people

We have never lost an American in space; we are sure as (heck) not going to lose one on my watch. Failure is not an option

I don't care what anything was designed to do. I care about what it can do

With all due respect sir, I think this is going to be our finest hour

As the scientists tried to figure out the solution to the problems, Kranz made them think outside the box. He always believed in the ability of his team. They broke down systems and used different parts to create new tools and systems that saved the lives of the crew. According to NASA (2009), 'The most remarkable achievement of mission control was quickly developing procedures for powering up the command module (CM) after its long, cold sleep. Flight controllers wrote the documents for this innovation in three days, instead of the usual three months'.

Though the mission never achieved its core objective of landing on the moon, many still believe it was successful. Its success is attributed to the fact that the crew members arrived safely, and most importantly every single person at Mission Control was instrumental in showing how team-work and effective leadership averted the greatest space disaster that may have occurred in 1970.

Questions

- Using the skill approach, evaluate the leadership of Gene Kranz?
- What was the most important leadership skill required for his success and why?

Behavioural Theory

The inconsistencies in the evidence for the trait theory led researchers to pay attention to what leaders actually do and not what they inherently possess. The focus of behavioural theory is on how leaders behave towards their subordinates in various contexts (Northouse 2010; Wright 1996).

There have been four pivotal studies on the behavioural theory on leadership. The first one was carried out in the early 1930s at Iowa State University by Kurt Lewin and his associates, which focused on the leadership style of managers (Lewin et al. 1939). In their study, they identified three leadership styles: the autocratic leadership style (which involves telling the employees what to do), the democratic leadership style (which encourages participation in decision-making) and the laissez-faire leadership style (which is a hands-off approach). The second group of studies were carried out at Ohio State University, which were done concurrently with the third group of studies at the University of Michigan (Kahn 1956). Based on the 'fruitlessness' (Northouse 2010, p. 70) of the results of trait studies, the Ohio State researchers decided to analyse how individuals acted when they led organisations. Using questionnaires, they identified behaviours that they grouped into two categories: initiating structure and consideration (Stogdill 1974). Initiating structure behaviour '...involves [a] leader's concern for accomplishing the task. The leader defines and structures his or her own role and the role of subordinates towards attainment of task goals' (Yukl 2010, p. 104), while consideration behaviours are '...essentially relationship behaviours and include camaraderie, respect, trust, and like between leaders and followers' (Northouse 2010, p. 70). The Ohio State University researchers viewed these two behaviours as being independent and distinct; hence, a leader could be competent both in terms of consideration and initiating structure behaviours. Their views contrasted with the findings of the University of Michigan researchers, who identified two types of leadership behaviour: employee orientation and production orientation (Northouse 2010). The University of Michigan researchers proposed that both behaviours were of the same continuum and not opposite forms, making the measurement one-dimensional (Lussier and Achua 2001; Northouse 2010); hence, leaders who are more oriented towards production will care less about the needs of their employees, and vice versa.

Studies carried out at the Ohio and Michigan universities laid the foundation for perhaps the most popular model of leadership behaviour, known as the Blake and Mouton managerial grid, and also referred to as the leadership grid (Daft 1999; Northouse 2010). Using the two-dimensional axes of concern for people and concern for tasks or results, leaders are grouped into five leadership styles: authority compliance (9, 1), country club management (1, 9), impoverished management (1, 1), middle of the road management (5, 5) and team management (9, 9). These different styles are described below:

- Authority Compliance (9, 1): This leader has a high concern for production and low concern for people. The emphasis is on getting work done at the expense of building good working relationships.
- Country Club Management (1, 9): This leader has a high concern for people and low concern for production. There is a good working environment but getting the task done is always secondary.
- Impoverished Management (1, 1): This leader has a low concern for people and production. There is a hands-off attitude and minimal effort on building relationships or getting the tasks completed.

- Middle of the Road Management (5, 5): This leader has a middle concern for production and people. There is a moderate effort to accomplish the tasks by creating a good working environment. However, the result is not optimum. It is more like a Jack of all Trades and master of none approach!
- Team Management (9, 9): This leader has a high concern for people and production. There is a very good working environment and relationship between the leaders and the employees but the focus still remains on achieving the organisational goals. It could be termed the Jack of all Trades and master of all approach!

Blake and Mouton (1985) argued that the most effective leader is the team manager who shows high concern for both tasks and people. However, the empirical basis for the grid has been criticised by various researchers (Gill 2011; Northouse 2010; Yukl 1999). As stated by Yukl (1999, p. 34), 'Studies on the implications of the two behaviours for leadership have not yielded consistent results. Survey studies using behaviour description questionnaires failed to provide much support for the idea that effective leaders have high scores on both dimensions'. In some situations, it may be necessary to adopt a more people-oriented perspective, while in other situations a task-oriented approach may be more effective.

Generally, studies into behavioural theory have failed to consider the situational contingencies associated with leadership. As with the trait research, the behavioural theory is limited on the basis of theory building and orientation (House and Aditya 1997; Yukl 1999). The task and relationship-based categories proposed in earlier studies do not include all types of leadership behaviour. Important behaviours that are relevant to understanding leadership (such as envisioning, leading by example, management of meaning and values) are absent (Gill 2011; Yukl 1999).

In conclusion, the behavioural theory has marked a major shift of focus in leadership research. However, as with the trait approach, it is plagued by inconsistencies in research results, and researchers have not been able to prove exactly how leadership styles are associated with performance outcomes (Gill 2011; Northouse 2010; Yukl 1999). The knowledge of the impact of situation and context in leadership, together with the inability of researchers to identify universal behaviours associated with effective leadership, led to the evolution of contingency theory.

Case Study 2.2

Leadership Style

Michael O'Leary is the CEO of Ryanair. He built a multibillion pound business and has shaped the airline industry. Budget airlines were not popular until O'Leary took the helm of affairs in 1994 from Tony Ryan who he served as an accountant.

The early Ryanair was not profitable and was run with the ideologies of the typical traditional airline. However, based on the Southwest airline model, he was able to create a new chapter for Ryanair. There was no longer business class. They stopped serving free meals and employees were made to work harder. Even the planes worked more by being used for more flights per day. This low-cost model was new in Europe. In order to reduce their cost, Ryanair uses small and isolated airports. They have been able to develop secondary airports that have not had significant traffic in the past. As a result, they are even able to rename those airports since they are almost the sole users. A good example is the Glasgow Prestwick Airport which used to be known as Prestwick Airport.

Ryanair has been profitable by ensuring that their planes are used to full capacity. They aggressively target customers by offering a price nobody in the industry can match. However, this has come at a cost. According to BBC (2013), employees are not even given pens for free, and O'Leary encourages his staff to go to hotels to get pens. Allegedly, his meetings with senior management are a war zone, and employees have even been reduced to tears. O'Leary denies this in his interview with the BBC (2013) but agrees that there is no 'hand-holding' in his meetings. Despite the aggression and tears, managers still work for him and many believe they have developed better under his leadership.

In ensuring that Ryanair keeps up with its low-cost and low-fare model, Michael O'Leary does not use advertising agencies. He is very media frenzy and uses any opportunity to get publicity. He seeks controversy as a form of advertising. For him, all publicity is good publicity. Even detrimental court cases are considered good news by O'Leary. BBC News (2009) quotes that O'Leary has said that he wants to charge a higher fare for fat people. He is also quoted to have said he intends to charge for the use of toilets in the plane. However, it is arguable that he uses all these comments to generate free publicity.

Unlike other airlines, Michael O'Leary does not believe that friendliness to the customer is important. His vision is to achieve the lowest fare possible no matter the cost, and so it is not surprising that customers repeatedly complain about the service rendered. Despite all the controversy and complaints, Ryanair is doing very well and is worth 14 billion euros (Independent 2015). Customers are able to fly at very cheap rates compared to some years ago. Family ties are now stronger, and secluded cities are now more popular thanks to Ryanair and of course Michael O'Leary.

Questions

- What is the leadership style of Michael O'Leary?
- What could be the consequence of taking his style too far?

Contingency Theory

Due to weaknesses in past research findings concerning leader behaviours and effectiveness, scholars moved towards a contingency theory in an effort to redress the shortcomings of the behavioural theory (Cogliser and Brigham 2004). The contingency theory proposes that there is no optimum style of leadership. Effective leaders will use different styles based on the contingencies of the situation; hence, a style of leadership which was ideal in the past might not be of great use in the present. This model to leadership has appealed to many researchers, the most prominent of whom is Fiedler, who proposed the contingency theory in the late 1960s (Gill 2011). Fiedler's (1978) theory suggests that leadership effectiveness depends on how well the personality of the leader fits the situation or context. Fiedler proposed the least preferred co-worker (LPC) scale, with which the personality of the leader could be measured as being relationship-motivated or task-motivated. Fiedler (1978) suggested that situational favourableness can be characterised by leader–member relations, task structure and position power. A situation is highly favourable when there is a good relationship between the leader and the group, a clear-cut structure, and when the leader has strong position power. On the other hand, a situation is least favourable when there are poor leader–member relations, unstructured tasks and weak leader position power (Fiedler 1997; Gill 2011; Northouse 2010). Based on their findings, it is said that people who are task-motivated (i.e. low LPC score) will be suited for highly favourable and unfavourable conditions, while those that are relationship-motivated (i.e. high LPC score) will be more effective in moderately favourable situations (Fiedler 1978, 1997). The contingency theory proposed by Fiedler does not require that leaders be effective in every situation; instead, only those who are ideal for that situation should be allowed to lead, and a leader with the wrong attributes could cause an operation to fail.

The contingency theory-based research carried out by Fiedler has also been criticised for inconsistent results (Gill 2011; Northouse 2010; Wright 1996; Yukl 2010). It is difficult to validate the findings of the Fiedler model (Yukl 2010), as they are built on the measurement of leadership style using the LPC scale, which itself has not been validated. Although Fiedler's model has broadened scholars' knowledge and understanding of leadership by bringing situation into perspective, it fails to explain why people with certain leadership styles are more effective in particular contexts than others (Northouse 2010). Fiedler's approach concerned task-oriented and relationship-oriented leaders while later research has shown that most leaders have a balance of both behaviours. As stated by Yukl (2010, p. 168), 'The model (and most of the research) neglects medium LPC leaders, who probably outnumber the high and low LPC leaders. Research suggests that medium LPC leaders are more effective than high or low LPC leaders in a majority of situations (five of the eight octants), presumably because they balance concern for the tasks and concern for relationships more successfully'.

In conclusion, the contingency theory has highlighted that situation needs to be considered when assessing leadership behaviour. In a world plagued with change, the idea that leaders in organisations must be able to adapt their behaviour to meet different situations is important. Despite their contribution, early contingency theories possessed many conceptual weaknesses that made these theories difficult to validate and use (Yukl 2011). The ambiguity of findings in relation to the early contingency theories led to a wane in scholarly interest (House and Aditya 1997; Yukl 2011). Scholars turned their attention to other approaches, and these approaches are the emerging paradigms which will be discussed in the next chapter.

Summary

This chapter examined and evaluated the different early approaches and theories of leadership. The Great Man theory focuses on heroic individuals, implying that only a selected few can achieve greatness. The trait theory conceptualises leadership on the universality of some given attributes. The skill theory focuses on the abilities of a leader. Behavioural theory views leaders based on their actions and behaviour, while the contingency theory concerns the context of leadership. The shortcomings and limitations of these different theories, which have led to newer approaches to leadership, were also examined.

Note

1. A theory is a "…statement of concepts and their interrelationships that shows how and/or why a phenomenon occurs" (Corley and Gioia 2011, p. 12).

References

Appelbaum, S. H., Audet, L., & Miller, J. C. (2003). Gender and leadership? Leadership and gender? A journey through the landscape of theories. *Leadership & Organization Development Journal, 24*(1), 43–51.

Bass, B. M. (1990). *Bass and Stogdills handbook of leadership*. New York: Free Press.

Bass, B. M., & Bass, R. (2009). *The Bass handbook of leadership: Theory, research, and managerial applications* (4th ed.). New York: Free Press.

BBC. (2013). *Flights and fights: Inside the low cost airlines documentary*. United Kingdom: BBC Two.

BBC News. (2009). *Ryanair mulls charge for toilets*. http://news.bbc.co.uk/1/hi/7914542.stm. Accessed 12 June 2017.

Blake, R. R., & Mouton, J. S. (1985). *The managerial grid III*. Houston, Texas: Gulf Publishing Company.

Cogliser, C. C., & Brigham, K. H. (2004). The intersection of leadership and entrepreneurship: Mutual lessons to be learned. *The Leadership Quarterly, 15*(6), 771–799.

Corley, K. G., & Gioia, D. A. (2011). Building theory about theory building: What constitutes a theoretical contribution? *Academy of Management Review, 36*(1), 12–32.

Daft, R. L. (1999). *Leadership theory and practice*. Orlando: The Dryden Press, Harcourt Brace College Publishers.

Denmark, F. L. (1993). Women, leadership, and empowerment. *Psychology of Women Quarterly, 17*(3), 343–356.

Dinh, J. E., Lord, R. G., Gardner, W. L., Meuser, J. D., Liden, R. C., & Hu, J. (2014). Leadership theory and research in the new millennium: Current theoretical trends and changing perspectives. *The Leadership Quarterly, 25*(1), 36–62.

Fiedler, F. E. (1978). The contingency model and the dynamics of the leadership process. In L. Berkowitz (Ed.), *Advances in the experimental social psychology* (pp. 59–112). New York: Academic Press.

Fiedler, F. E. (1997). Situational control and a dynamic theory of leadership. In K. Grint (Ed.), *Leadership. Classical, contemporary, and critical approaches* (pp. 126–148). Oxford: Oxford University Press.

Gill, R. (2011). *Theory and practice of leadership* (2nd ed.). London: Sage.

Grazer, B. (Producer), & Howard, R. (Director). (1995). *Apollo 13* [Motion picture]. United Kingdom: Universal Pictures.

Grint, K. (2011). A history of leadership. In A. Bryman, D. Collinson, K. Grint, B. Jackson, & M. Uhl-Bien (Eds.), *The Sage handbook of leadership* (pp. 1–14). London: Sage.

House, R. J., & Aditya, R. N. (1997). The social scientific study of leadership: Quo vadis? *Journal of Management, 23*(3), 409–473.

Independent. (2015). *Ryanair worth €14bn as share rise sends O'Leary's wealth Skywards.* http://www.independent.ie/irish-news/ryanair-worth-14bn-as-share-rise-sends-olearys-wealth-skywards-30885019.html. Accessed 12 June 2017.

Kahn, R. L. (1956). The prediction of productivity. *Journal of Social Issues, 12*(2), 41–49.

Katz, R. L. (1955). Skills of an effective administrator. *Harvard Business Review, 33*(1), 33–42.

Kolb, J. A. (1999). The effect of gender role, attitude toward leadership, and self-confidence on leader emergence: Implications for leadership development. *Human Resource Development Quarterly, 10*(4), 305–320.

Lewin, K., Lippert, R., & White, R. K. (1939). Patterns of aggressive behavior in experimentally created social climates. *Journal of Social Psychology, 10*(2), 271–301.

Lord, R. C., De Vader, C. L., & Alliger, G. M. (1986). A meta-analysis of the relation between personality traits and leadership perceptions: An application of validity generalization procedures. *Journal of Applied Psychology, 71*(3), 402–410.

Lussier, R. N., & Achua, C. F. (2001). *Leadership: Theory, application & skill development.* Cincinnati, OH: South Western College Publishing, Thomson learning.

Mann, R. D. (1959). A review of the relationship between personality and performance in small groups. *Psychological Bulletin, 56*(4), 241–270.

McClelland, D. C. (1965). N achievement and entrepreneurship: A longitudinal study. *Journal of Personality and Social Psychology, 1*(4), 389–392.

McClelland, D. C. (1975). *Power: The inner experience.* New York: Irvington.

McClelland, D. C. (1985). *Human motivation.* Glenview, IL: Scott, Foresman.

Mumford, M. D., Zaccaro, S. J., Harding, F. D., Jacobs, T. O., & Fleishman, E. A. (2000a). Leadership skills for a changing world solving complex social problems. *The Leadership Quarterly, 11*(1), 11–35.

Mumford, M. D., Marks, M. A., Connelly, M. S., Zaccaro, S. J., & Reiter-Palmon, R. (2000b). Development of leadership skills: Experience and timing. *The Leadership Quarterly, 11*(1), 87–114.

NASA. (2009). *Apollo 13.* https://www.nasa.gov/mission_pages/apollo/missions/apollo13.html. Accessed 12 June 2017.

Northouse, P. G. (2010). *Leadership: Theory and practice* (5th ed.). Thousand Oaks: CA: Sage.

Oakley, J. G. (2000). Gender-based barriers to senior management positions: Understanding the scarcity of female CEOs. *Journal of Business Ethics, 27*(4), 321–334.

Powell, G. N., & Graves, L. M. (2003). *Women and men in management* (3rd ed.). Thousand Oaks, CA: Sage.

Shimanoff, S. B., & Jenkins, M. M. (1991). Leadership and gender: Challenging assumptions and recognizing resources. In R. S. Cathcart & L. A. Samovar (Eds.), *Small group communication: A reader* (pp. 504–522). Dubuque, IA: W. C. Brown.

Spector, B. A. (2016). Carlyle, freud, and the great man theory more fully considered. *Leadership, 12*(2), 250–260.

Stogdill, R. M. (1948). Personal factors associated with leadership: A survey of the literature. *Journal of Psychology, 25*(1), 35–71.

Stogdill, R. M. (1974). *Handbook of leadership*. New York: Free Press.

Van Wart, M. (2003). Public-sector leadership theory: An assessment. *Public Administration Review, 63*(2), 214–229.

Wright, P. (1996). *Managerial leadership*. London: Routledge.

Yukl, G. (1999). An evaluative essay on current conceptions of effective leadership. *European Journal of Work & Organizational Psychology, 8*(1), 33–48.

Yukl, G. (2010). *Leadership in organisations* (7th ed.). Upper Saddle River, NJ: Pearson Education Limited.

Yukl, G. (2011). Contingency theories of effective leadership. In A. Bryman, D. Collinson, K. Grint, B. Jackson, & M. Uhl-Bien (Eds.), *The Sage handbook of leadership* (pp. 286–298). London: Sage.

3

Emerging Paradigms

Abstract After the contingency theory of leadership, theorists began to develop alternative approaches to understanding leadership. The new approaches to leadership are discussed in this chapter. These new approaches to leadership are implicit leadership theories, leader–member exchange, servant, charismatic, transactional, transformational, distributed, authentic and entrepreneurial leadership. Case studies are available to assess the reader's understanding of the relevant approaches in this chapter. This chapter argues that leadership is an underdeveloped phenomenon, for which no unified theory currently exists. The strengths and weaknesses of these approaches are listed and discussed.

Keywords Implicit leadership theories · Leader–member exchange Servant leadership · Charismatic leadership · Transformational leadership · Entrepreneurial leadership

© The Author(s) 2018
C. Harrison, *Leadership Theory and Research*,
https://doi.org/10.1007/978-3-319-68672-1_3

Introduction

After the contingency theory of leadership, theorists began to develop alternative approaches to understanding leadership. There was a renewed interest in the trait perspective (House and Aditya 1997; Wright 1996) and other alternative behavioural approaches (Wright 1996); hence, the theory of leadership after the mid-1970 was fragmented. The new approaches to leadership will be discussed in this chapter. These new approaches to leadership are implicit leadership theories, leader–member exchange, servant, charismatic, transactional, transformational, distributed, authentic and entrepreneurial leadership.

Implicit Leadership Theories

Just as leaders make attributions about their follower's ability and competence, followers in turn make attributions about the expected behaviour and traits of their leaders (Yukl 2010). The implicit leadership theories represent a shift to an attributional perspective on leadership. Leadership is viewed subjectively from the lens of the followers. It involves leadership as a permanent entrenched part of the socially constructed reality by individuals; it is, therefore, a romanticised conception of leadership by those who are led (Meindl et al. 1985). The conceptualisation of implicit leadership theory is based on the work of Calder (1977) (see Lord et al. 1982; Lord et al. 1984; Lord and Maher 1993; Phillips and Lord 1981), who proposed an attribution theory of leadership, in which followers use information based on a leader's actions and performance to reach conclusions about the competence of their leader. The implicit leadership theories represent a shift in focus, from the traits and behaviour of leaders, towards addressing how individuals perceive their leaders and the cognitive processes of the evaluation of their leaders. Lord and Maher (1991, p. 11) refer to leadership '… as a process of being perceived by others as a leader'. Hence, they put forward the notion that no matter what traits or behaviours are present in an individual, if the subordinates do not perceive a person to be a leader, then the individual is not a leader. Lord and Maher (1993) argue that the perception of leadership by the followers is dependent on the traits and behaviour identified by them as well as the outcomes produced by their leaders. For example, an individual who is courageous, intelligent and assertive could be regarded as a good leader, based on the followers' innate perception of these traits as being important for leadership. In addition, positive performance outcomes by the leader will also foster followers' perception that leaders possess such traits.

However, implicit leadership theories also have limitations that need to be considered, one of which is the validity of the method. The credibility of implicit leadership theories is affected by biased ratings in leadership behaviour questionnaires (Yukl 2010). Researchers such as Bryman (1987) have expressed concern about the validity and meaning of the questionnaire measures. As stated by Yukl (2010, p. 249), 'When relevant and irrelevant aspects of behaviour are confounded in the same questionnaire, it is difficult to interpret the results from research that uses it'.

In conclusion, implicit leadership theories represent a major shift from actual leadership behaviour to perceived leadership behaviour. They acknowledge the importance of the social construction of leadership by the followers. However, irrational observers will hold biased perceptions of leadership performance.

Leader–Member Exchange Theory

Most of the early theories on leadership focused on leader's behaviours and traits, or on the follower and the context in which leadership is enacted. The leader–member exchange theory takes a psychodynamic approach by conceptualising leadership based on the relationship and interaction between leaders and followers. The approach was proposed by Graen and his colleagues (Dansereau et al. 1975; Graen and Cashman 1975), and was originally referred to as the vertical dyad linkage theory (VDL). The basic premise of this theory is that leaders develop different types of relationships with individual group members which are known as dyads. Graen and Cashman (1975) proposed that subordinates are members of either an in-group or an out-group. The in-group members develop a close relationship with the leader based on trust, respect, negotiation and mutual influence (Dansereau et al. 1975; Graen and Uhl-Bien 1995; Liden and Maslyn 1998). The out-group members do not possess a close relationship with the leader; rather, the relationship is transactional, bound to employment contracts, and characterised by low trust, respect and obligation (Graen and Uhl-Bien 1995). Therefore, subordinates make their way into in-groups by doing extra work for their managers, while the out-group members do little more than that which is specified for their jobs (or to use a colloquial phrase, 'the bare minimum').

Research findings on leader–member exchange and its impact on an organisation have also been plagued by inconsistencies and contradictory results. As stated by House and Aditya (1997, p. 433), 'However, closer scrutiny indicates that empirical findings relating LMX (leader–member exchange) to dependent variables are mixed and less supportive of the theory than Graen and Uhl-Bien imply'. Controversy still surrounds the authenticity and efficacy of the leader–member exchange theory (see Gill 2011; House and Aditya 1997; Northouse 2010; Wright 1996; Yukl 2010). A prominent issue in this respect is the validity of the leader–member exchange scale that is used to measure the relationship between leaders and followers. The issue of discrimination and equality has also been a bone of contention. Works by Scandura (1999) and Sias and Jablin (1995) show that differentiating subordinates into in-groups and out-groups could be detrimental to the effectiveness of the organisation and may lead to conflict.

Case Study 3.1

Leader–Member Exchange

George Brown is the Chief Operating Officer (COO) of Rivler Enterprises. Rivler is a manufacturing company that specialises in the production of metal components used in automobiles. He has been in this position for five years. However, prior to his elevation as the COO, he served as the production supervisor for five years and later as the production manager for another eight years.

Most of the employees are happy to work in Rivler. They attest that the atmosphere is positive and the leadership of George has been instrumental to their success. Nevertheless, George does not delegate responsibilities to everybody in the organisation. In his 18 year period in the company, he has grown to trust three employees, Laura, Charles and Victory. These three employees have always delivered effectively and on time. Most of the customers they presently have were recruited by Laura and Victory, while Charles is the brain behind the innovative designs they churn out yearly.

However, some of the employees feel left out in the organisation. Although they are generally satisfied, they believe that their input is not recognised. An employee whose name is John wants additional responsibilities. He feels that George does not trust him even though he has worked in the company for seven years.

At present, Rivler is doing well but the future outlook might change if staff such as John persists with such concern.

Questions

- Using the leader–member exchange theory can you assess George's leadership examining the in-groups and out-groups?
- Do you think his approach to delegation will remain effective in Rivler in times ahead and why?

* This is a fictional case. Names, characters, places and incidents either are products of the author's imagination or are used fictitiously. Any resemblance to actual persons, living or dead, or actual events is purely coincidental.

Servant Leadership Theory

Servant leadership theory represents a radical shift from the perception of a leader as an all-knowing individual to that of a selfless servant. There is an increasing concern in management research that in order to succeed as an organisation, people need to be empowered, and the long-term welfare of the followers must come first (Smith et al. 2004; Yukl 2010). This is the basis of servant leadership. Servant leadership itself is a paradoxical concept because people view servants and leaders as entirely different people, and it can be difficult to conceptualise an individual as being both at the same time.

The root of this type of leadership is grounded in the works of Greenleaf (1977). According to Greenleaf (1998, p. 19),

> The servant-leader is servant first... It begins with the natural feeling that one wants to serve, to serve first. Then conscious choices bring one to aspire to lead. That person is sharply different from one who is leader first, perhaps because of the need to assuage an unusual power or to acquire material possessions.

According to Greenleaf, servant leaders put their service before self-interest, earn trust by being trustworthy, help others to discover themselves and listen actively to the problems of the group rather than impose their will on others (Daft 1999). The focus of this type of leadership is similar to stewardship and has been used synonymously with spiritual leadership (Sendjaya and Sarros 2002). However, unlike stewardship (which involves empowerment of employees), servant leadership goes further and calls for the highest level of selflessness (Lussier and Achua 2001). There has been increased interest in the acceptance of the servant leadership theory proposed by Greenleaf (e.g. Russell and Stone 2002; Sendjaya and Sarros 2002; Smith et al. 2004; Spears 1998). Spears (1998) identified ten characteristics of a servant leader:

- Listening
- Empathy
- Healing
- Awareness
- Persuasion
- Conceptualisation
- Foresight
- Stewardship

- Commitment to the growth of people
- Community building

Russell and Stone (2002, p. 147) go further and identify 20 attributes that are important in servant leadership. These are categorised into functional attributes (which are identifiable characteristics necessary to enact leadership responsibilities, e.g. vision, honesty, integrity, trust, service, modelling, pioneering, appreciation of others and empowerment) and accompanying attributes (which supplement the functional attributes, e.g. communication, credibility, competence, stewardship, visibility, influence, persuasion, listening, encouragement, teaching and delegation).

Many researchers have argued that servant leadership is essential for organisational success. Smith et al. (2004) contrasted transformational and servant leadership, and proposed that servant leadership is more effective than transformational leadership in stable environments such as non-profit, voluntary and religious organisations. They also argued that the efficacy of servant leadership is based on the life cycle stage of the organisation. At the maturity stage, when concern for employees and personal growth is paramount, servant leadership is the most effective form of leadership. A lack of servant leadership will create a dysfunctional, unproductive job environment (Bausch 1998). Sendjaya and Sarros (2002) examined the philosophical foundation of servant leadership and suggested that servant leaders take on both the role and nature of a servant. They rebutted the claim by other researchers that servant leadership is not ideal in organisations, by stating that it exists and will continue to do so.

Although this type of leadership has been recognised in literature, there is insufficient empirical evidence available which can justify its validity. Yukl (2010) argues that most evidence about the impact of servant leadership consists of anecdotal accounts and case studies of historical leaders. Most accounts are descriptive and have not been tested by qualitative or quantitative research methodologies (Northouse 2010). As a result, researchers have developed different constructs to define servant leadership (e.g. Barbuto and Wheeler 2006; Laub et al. 1999; Liden et al. 2008; and Page and Wong 2000). The numerous constructs developed are proof that researchers conceptualise and measure servant leadership differently, which only increases the need for a uniform approach to measuring the phenomenon.

The efficacy of servant leadership in all settings has aroused controversy among researchers. Gill (2011) argues that servant leadership theories ignore the many demands that an organisation presents, especially in business where stakeholders' welfare and satisfaction comes before the interests of the employees. Servant leadership also fails to explain clearly how such a leader will cope when drastic measures such as downsizing have to be carried out to improve organisational performance (Yukl 2010). With organisations needing to cope with change and increasing turbulence, servant leadership may not be suitable in a dynamic context, although Russell and Stone (2002, p. 154) state that, 'Servant leadership is a concept that potentially change organisations and societies because it stimulates both personal and organisational metamorphosis'. Research has shown that servant leadership may only be suitable in stable environments such as religious institutions and may not be effective in more dynamic contexts (e.g. Smith et al. 2004); hence, future research is required to clarify how servant leadership could influence followers and the ideal situation that guarantees its efficacy.

Case Study 3.2

Servant Leadership

Charles Harry is the Chief Executive Officer (CEO) of an information technology (IT) service company. His company specialises in providing IT services to higher education institutions. The company has grown vastly in the last 20 years. The company started as a one-man business with an entrepreneurial structure but has greatly expanded and is located in different countries in the world.

However, during the recession in 2008, the profit of the company started to dwindle. It was clear that they had to refocus and like many others downsize. Rumours were being circulated around the company that five out of 10 employees would lose their jobs. The staff were already coming up with contingency plans and some had started searching aggressively for other jobs. Surprisingly, contrary to the rumours, Charles assured all the staff that no job would be lost. He understood that there were tough times ahead but he believed that by sticking together, they could go beyond it. He was willing to share their pains and this he did by reducing his salary so that he could afford to pay others.

Before he embarked on his cost-cutting venture especially with expenses in the organisation, he established a group and empowered them to come up with the best decisions to move the company forward. This was instrumental and made his employees trust him. His company was able to survive the storm in 2008, and in 2017, it has become a larger and more sought-after brand.

Questions

- What makes Charles Harry a servant leader?
- Based on the characteristics proposed by Spears (1998) and Russell and Stone (2002) for servant leadership, what are the attributes that Charles Harry possesses?
- What are the benefits of his approach to leadership?
- Are there negative consequences of focusing on the welfare of his employees rather than the company's performance?

* This is a fictional case. Names, characters, places and incidents either are products of the author's imagination or are used fictitiously. Any resemblance to actual persons, living or dead, or actual events is purely coincidental.

Charismatic Leadership Theory

After many years of comparative neglect, there has been a resurgence of interest in both traits and behavioural aspects of leadership in the form of charismatic leadership. The word 'charisma' is a Greek word that means a gift of God's grace or divine power (Conger 2011, p. 87). The current theories of charismatic leadership were strongly influenced by Max Weber. According to Weber (1947), charisma occurs when a leader emerges with a radical vision that offers solution to a crisis or problem and, as a result, enables followers to believe in the vision (Yukl 2010). Following the work of Weber, several theorists proposed versions of theories concerning charismatic leadership in organisations (e.g. Conger and Kanungo 1987, 1998; House 1977). For Conger and Kanungo (1987, 1998), charisma is an attribute based on the follower's perception of their leader's behaviour. The leader's qualities of dynamism, strategic insight, vision and the ability to motivate are important traits that appear as extraordinary to subordinates, who in turn show a natural inclination towards them (Wright 1996). Charismatic leaders empower their subordinates by providing opportunities to accomplish difficult tasks. For Conger and Kanungo (1998), charismatic leaders are not autocratic but inspire with emotional appeal. They identify opportunities that others have failed to recognise and exploit, and thus endear their followers to them. House (1977), a proponent of charismatic leadership in organisations, outlined the leadership behaviours, traits and situational variables associated with charismatic leadership. He suggested that charismatic leaders are self-confident and have a strong conviction in their own abilities and beliefs. These leaders also have the ability to dominate and influence others. House (1977) theorised that charismatic leaders communicate high expectations for their followers as well as confidence in their subordinates' abilities to meet them. In concert with Weber, House contends that charismatic leadership is seen in settings marked by distress where subordinates feel the need for someone to come to their aid. As with many leadership theories, House's (1977) theory had its shortcomings. Important components of charismatic leadership such as self-sacrifice and unconventional behaviour were omitted, with leadership being viewed more as a dyadic process than as a collective one (Conger 2011). This led to a revision of House's theory by Shamir et al. (1993), who proposed that through charismatic leadership, followers' self-concepts could be transformed by the use of intrinsic rewards. Followers should view their work as an expression of themselves and identify collectively with the organisation. For Shamir et al. (1993), charismatic leadership relates to personal and social identification with the leader and internalisation of the leader's values.

Charismatic leadership theory makes an important contribution to the study of leadership by emphasising the importance of the influence of leaders on their followers. However, charismatic leadership theory has been heavily criticised (House and Aditya 1997; Wright 1996; Yukl 2010). It is built on the emergence of leadership under crisis, but businesses are not always facing a crisis. The concept of charismatic leadership stemmed from the observation of symbolic figures and great leaders such as Winston Churchill, Martin Luther King and a host of other leaders; however, research on charismatic leadership has failed to distinguish between positive and negative charisma. Can Adolf Hitler be said to be a charismatic leader? As with early trait theories, charisma is an 'all or nothing matter' (Wright 1996, p. 212)—one either has it or does not.

Case Study 3.3

Charismatic Leadership

John was faced with a big issue. His father's chain of restaurants was no longer profitable. This was his father's legacy and he had promised him on his death bed that he would not sell the company. However, for the last five years, the restaurants have not produced profit. John has had to use his personal funds to pay his employees. Most of his employees had worked for his father and were more like family. The change was indeed vital if the company was to progress beyond the year.

John had a college class mate; Chris who he worked with after graduation in an audit firm. In college, Chris was very charismatic and loved by all his classmates. He was the president of the students' body and was a popular figure in college. This did not change even when they worked together after college. Their line manager was always impressed with the way Chris handled situations and was very meticulous in his dealings. Nevertheless, Chris left the firm many years before John joined his father in his business. He owned several businesses which though small were striving.

John believed that Chris may be able to provide the solution to the problem he was facing. He contacted Chris and offered him the position of the Chief Operating Officer of the company with a lucrative package. Chris took up the position and went to work immediately.

Chris's arrival into the company sparked a lot of conversation and rumours among the employees. His leadership style was unique. They were used to a paternal approach adopted by John's father and later John. Their welfare has always been the focus. His first meeting with all the staff was very inspirational. He told them that the performance was going to improve within the next six months. The employees were sceptical about this because of the bad trend in performance in recent times. Nevertheless, they were prepared to work hard and meet the targets set out.

Chris was always the first to get to work and the last to leave. Employees had noticed this and their work attitude had changed. The work place had become so lively, and his personality and drive had affected all the employees. Nevertheless, the work place was still challenging, and Chris was the first to push the employees to meet the set objectives. Six months after, John did not know what Chris actually did. The performance of the company had improved dramatically. It was clear that the company has been transformed and the employees were more motivated and aligned with the goals of the organisation.

Questions

- Based on the charismatic leadership theory proposed by Weber (1947), will you classify Chris as a charismatic leader?
- What are the qualities of Chris that were important in restoring viability to the company?
- What are the negative consequences of the charismatic approach adopted by Chris?

* This is a fictional case. Names, characters, places and incidents either are products of the author's imagination or are used fictitiously. Any resemblance to actual persons, living or dead, or actual events is purely coincidental.

Transactional Leadership Theory

Transactional leadership is deeply rooted in the notion of the path goal theory, which is based on contingent rewards. The transactional theory was introduced by Burns (1978) and has been influential ever since (Gavan O' Shea et al. 2009).

A transactional leader motivates followers through exchanges that appeal to their self-interests. According to Bass (1985), transactional leadership involves contingent rewards and management-by-exception. Contingent rewards involve the use of incentives to motivate subordinates. Followers are made aware of the standard of performance expected and the rewards that they can obtain once they meet the necessary standards. Management-by-exception, a concept which was later modified in subsequent research by Bass and Avolio (1990), can either be active or passive. In the active form, the leader seeks out mistakes while watching the followers and enforces rules or takes coercive action to deter followers from making subsequent mistakes (Northouse 2010; Yukl 2010). With the passive form, the leader only intervenes after errors have occurred (hence, taking a passive approach).

A major source of controversy surrounding transactional leadership theory is based on the use of contingent rewards to influence subordinates. As stated by Gill (2011, p. 83) '… while this can result in short term achievement, it runs the risk of stifling human development, with the consequent loss of competitive advantage'. It should be noted, however, that subsequent research by scholars has shown that contingent rewards are valuable in enhancing job attitude and organisational effectiveness (Bass 1985; Gavan O'Shea et al. 2009). But although transactional leadership has been particularly effective in business settings (Judge and Piccolo 2004), there still remains an argument about its usefulness in diverse entrepreneurial settings.

Case Study 3.4

Transactional Leadership

Laura Abraham was recruited by a fast food company to manage their branch in New Orleans. Prior to her employment, labour productivity was low. There was no fixed process available. The waiting time for customers was high. They had developed the reputation of a place you go to when you have nothing urgent to do. When customers were served, it was the role of one employee to ensure that all the needs of the customer were met.

Laura believed that the structure in place was the root cause of the problem. Similar to the reasoning of Taylor, the father of scientific management, she believed that there has to be precise procedures developed to increase efficiency. She came up with specific plans to break the tasks, and labour was divided among the employees. It was no longer one employee doing all, but others contributed to the production process for the same customer.

She created an incentive system that paid each employee £50 commission for exceeding the target by 50% at the end of the month. In the same vein, she was regarded as the iron lady because she also ensured that those who do not meet the target in the first month were queried. If the same person fails to improve after three months, the individual was at the risk of losing his or her job. This did not sit well with the employees because they were not used to such high-performance culture. Regardless, they all worked hard to ensure that they met her expectation.

Productivity at the company shot up overnight, and it is arguable that it is the leadership approach adopted by Laura that made this possible.

Questions

- What type of leadership approach did Laura adopt in running the fast food establishment?
- According to Bass (1985), transactional leadership involves contingent rewards and management-by-exception. Were those two features prominent in her leadership approach? If so explain?
- What are the advantages of the leadership approach adopted by Laura?
- What are the disadvantages of the leadership approach adopted by Laura?

* This is a fictional case. Names, characters, places and incidents either are products of the author's imagination or are used fictitiously. Any resemblance to actual persons, living or dead, or actual events is purely coincidental.

Transformational Leadership Theory

During the 1970s and 1980s, when the environment confronting many organisations became more turbulent, researchers became more interested in how leadership could effect change. This focus led to the development of what has become known as transformational leadership. For the past 30 years, transformational leadership has been the most debated and studied aspect in the domain of leadership (Diaz-Saenz 2011). The phrase 'transformational leadership' was first coined by Dowton in 1973 (Diaz-Saenz 2011; Northouse 2010), but as with transactional leadership, it was Burns (1978) who brought it to wide prominence in his book, *Leadership*. At the same time, during when Burns proposed the theory of transformational leadership, House (1977) published his theory on charismatic leadership. These approaches to leadership are often considered to be synonymous (Northouse 2010).

For Burns (1978) and Bass (1985), transformational leadership involves stimulating followers to go beyond their self-interests in order to achieve organisational goals or objectives. Using a multifactor leadership questionnaire (MLQ), Bass (1985) developed a model for transformational leadership consisting of behaviours, namely, idealised influence, inspirational motivation, intellectual stimulation and individualised consideration.

- Idealised influence: Leaders are viewed as role models by their followers. They are respected and admired. Followers emulate and trust them. They are perceived by their followers as pedestals of exemplary behaviour.
- Inspirational motivation: Leaders behave in a way that inspire and motivate their followers. They convey their expectations to their

followers clearly and challenge them to meet the set organisational goals.

- Intellectual stimulation: Leaders stimulate their followers to be creative and innovative. They ensure that their followers do not take everything at face value. They encourage them to question assumptions and challenge the status quo. New ideas and creativity are rewarded, and failure due to new approaches is not punished.
- Individualised consideration: Leaders treat their followers differently and do not assume that they have the same needs. There is a specific focus on each follower's growth. By identifying the individual's needs, the leader takes up the role of a mentor and can identify learning opportunities to foster personal growth.

In addition to the model of transformational leadership proposed by Bass (1985) and Bass and Avolio (1994) (with modifications by other researchers), several other scholars have tried to redefine transformational leadership by incorporating vision which has led to the concept of visionary leadership (e.g. Bennis and Nanus 1985; Kouzes and Posner 1987, 2002).

Empirical research has shown that transformational leadership behaviours have a favourable effect on followers' performance and satisfaction (Dionne et al. 2004). Nevertheless, as with extant theories of leadership, conceptual weaknesses and limitations have been observed by researchers (e.g. Diaz-Saenz 2011; Gill 2011; Northouse 2010; Wright 1996; Yukl 2010). Though the validity of the MLQ in assessing transformational leadership has been confirmed by many researchers (e.g. Judge and Piccolo 2004; Lowe et al. 1996; Yammarino et al. 1993), Carless (1998) proposed that it assesses only a single construct and is not valuable in measuring distinct transformational leadership behaviours. This stance was supported by Podsakoff et al. (1990), and as a result, these researchers developed their own scale for measuring transformational leadership.

Furthermore, transformational leadership theory tends to give much credit to the leader, at the expense of other factors (Diaz-Saenz 2011). Transformational leadership has been seen as a 'better' approach than transactional leadership, resulting in the latter being viewed more negatively (Dionne et al. 2004). However, studies have shown that transactional leadership may be a more effective style in stable and predictable environments (Lowe et al. 1996). In business and entrepreneurial settings, the role of contingent rewards in motivating staff members may be appropriate.

In conclusion, transformational leadership provides leaders with a broader view of the behaviours necessary for effectiveness. However, a more rigorous research is required to determine how these behaviours may improve subordinates' responses and organisational effectiveness.

Case Study 3.5

Transformational Leadership

Steve Jobs was the co-founder, Chairman and Chief Executive Officer (CEO) of Apple before his death. Apart from Apple, he was an important stakeholder in Pixar, Walt Disney and NeXT. He is widely regarded as the pioneer of the smartphone industry.

Apple was co-founded with Steve Wozniak in 1976. Apple 1 was the first of many computers to follow. The success of their inventions enabled them break into Silicon Valley, and Jobs had become very successful and wealthy at a very young age. Steve Jobs was able to persuade John Scully away from Pepsi Cola to assume the position of Apple CEO. His persuasive words to John have since become popular. 'Do you want to spend the rest of your life selling sugared water, or do you want a chance to change the world?' It is believed that it was those words that made John leave Pepsi Cola to Apple despite the illustrious position he occupied in Pepsi Cola.

However, by 1985, the working relationship between Scully and Jobs had deteriorated significantly. Scully did not like the decisions made by Jobs and felt it was detrimental to the company. As a result, Wozniak left Apple and sold out his stock. Scully proposed a restructure of Apple and the removal of Jobs from the Mackintosh group but putting him in charge of product development. This move did not go well with Jobs, and instead, he plotted the removal of Scully. The plot was later unravelled, and this led to his resignation from the company he co-founded on 17 September 1985.

Jobs was not deterred but started a new venture NeXT. This led to other ventures such as Pixar. In 1996, Jobs was back to Apple through the purchase of NeXT and assumed the role of CEO in 1997. Under Jobs guidance, Apple increased sales significantly with the introduction of products such as iMac, iPod portable music player, iTunes digital music software, iPad and a host of others. The most significant achievement of Apple can be said to be its entry into the cellular phone business with the introduction of the iPhone. This has since revolutionised mobile phone technology, and they arguably have the biggest share in the smartphone market.

Steve Jobs is perceived as a large-scale visionary and inventor (Issacson 2011). He is known for his meticulous and perfectionist stance. He invented the iPod in 2001 because he perceived that the existing music players were not good enough. IPhone came into existence because according to Issacson (2011) 'he noticed something odd about the cell phones on the market. They all stank, just like portable music players used to'.

Many have argued that Steve Jobs is more of a tweaker than an innovator (Gladwell 2011). Though he was able to transform the computer industry and was regarded as the number one CEO in America (Forbes 2012), he was more into tweaking than inventing. As stated by Gladwell (2011, p. 1) 'The visionary starts with a clean sheet of paper, and re-imagines the world. The tweaker inherits things as they are, and has to push and pull them toward some nearly perfect solution. That is not a lesser task'. He was very skilled in changing other people's ideas, and this led to controversies with Xerox, where he is said to have copied the major characteristic features of the Macintosh.

Nevertheless, Steve Jobs will always be remembered as the one whose products are at the fore front of information technology. His attention to detail, innovation and stylish trends will never be forgotten.

Questions

- What makes Steve Jobs a transformational leader?
- How important did Jobs vision for Apple play as a transformational leader?

Distributed Leadership Theory

Another way of conceptualising leadership that has emerged in recent years is that of distributed leadership. The term 'distributed leadership' has been used interchangeably with terms such as shared leadership, team leadership, participative leadership and democratic leadership by some researchers. It is a type of leadership that involves interaction between people and their situation (Spillane 2005). Leadership is dispersed among all members and is not merely a function of a single leader's action (Gronn 2002; Spillane 2005). Distributed leadership does not involve a single individual, but is a collective effort of the group. The traditional approach to understanding leadership examined it as a vertical process, whereby the individual's skills, traits or behaviour in different situations are important for effective leadership; hence, there has been much research on ways of improving the skills and behaviours, or on influencing the context. The proponents of distributed leadership argue that it is impossible for an individual to have all the skills and knowledge necessary for effective leadership (e.g. Gronn 2002; Harris 2004; Spillane et al. 2001). Followers, and the ways in which the leaders interact with them in different situations, must also be considered.

The construct of distributed leadership varies among different researchers. Some researchers view distributed leadership as an emergent property of a group or network of individuals (Gronn 2002), while others view it as either a democratic or autocratic process (Spillane 2005). The common theme among researchers is that distributed leadership does involve responsibilities being shared across a team, either formally or informally. Several authors have considered the impact of distributed leadership in organisational effectiveness (e.g. Ensley et al. 2006; Mehra et al. 2006; Pearce and Sims 2002) and have found a positive influence. In the field of entrepreneurship, distributed leadership has also been shown to be effective (e.g. Cope et al. 2011; Jones and Crompton 2009). Jones and Crompton (2009) provided empirical evidence to support a more distributed leadership approach by entrepreneurs. Cope et al. (2011) have gone further by exploring distributed leadership in a small business context, stressing the difficulty of its implementation.

In conclusion, researchers have shown that the orientation of small businesses makes the implementation of distributed leadership difficult. Therefore, it could be suggested that distributed leadership may not be feasible in every context, especially in small businesses where subordinates may resist empowerment.

Case Study 3.6

Distributed Leadership

Stellion High School is located in Lagos, Nigeria and the principal, Grace Peters has been in charge for over a decade. The school has been described by many individuals as a well-run establishment, and the model adopted is quite unique. In Stellion, the teachers assume most of the administrative roles. Grace believes that everyone in the school should have the opportunity to exercise leadership. Leadership is not restricted to her as the principal. She lets them deal with administrative issues and not only academic matters with students. The culture in Stellion is very accommodating. John who was just employed six months ago is already a school leader based on the identification of his capacity to lead.

However, the process of distributing these leadership roles is still in the hands of the principal. She identifies the individual that she believes fits the role required. For example; Sarah before her recruitment as a teacher had worked in human resource (HR) departments for many organisations. She decided to quit her role as an HR manager in those fast-paced establishments so that she could have more time for her young children. Grace had been struggling with human resources. To solve this problem, she appointed Sarah as the leader of the HR division and reduced her teaching work load. She also ensured that the flexibility that Sarah sought was still available by giving her more of an advisory role.

Furthermore, Grace has always known that there would be difficulty in successfully managing all the divisions of the school on her own. As a result, she ensured that she delegated responsibilities in other areas where she lacked the required expertise. In addition, a level of leadership was also mandatory for all staff. All staff had a level of leadership responsibility they must assume. In their job description as well as employment contract, a leadership responsibility is incorporated. The teachers were expected to lead at different levels. For example, the head of department position was just for two years and was rotated among every teacher in the department. So at a point, all the staff would have served as heads of their various departments. When everybody has served as the head, it is then rotated again. This practice has been lauded by many teachers as it has been able to build their confidence as well as their leadership ability.

Finally, the teachers are autonomous and Grace does not interfere in their roles. She ensures that they take ownership and empowers them. She trusts her teachers and their leadership capabilities. Her trust in them has been greatly repaid over the years. Her school has the highest teacher retention in the area, and the performance of the students over time has greatly improved. The parents of the students attest to their children's development and the quality of school life they receive. They are always happy to recommend other parents to Stellion.

Questions

- What type of leadership approach did Grace adopt in running Stellion?
- What are the benefits of this leadership approach?
- Is there a dark side to this approach and if so what are they?

* This is a fictional case. Names, characters, places and incidents either are products of the author's imagination or are used fictitiously. Any resemblance to actual persons, living or dead, or actual events is purely coincidental.

Authentic Leadership Theory

Authentic leadership research, which became widely recognised in 2003, '… has since attracted considerable theoretical attention and continues to figure prominently in practitioners' treatment of leadership' (Caza and Jackson 2011, p. 352). The scandals in companies such as Enron and in the banking sector have fuelled an increased interest in a leadership approach, which embodies integrity and increases trust within organisations. The result is a proposed theory of authentic leadership. In the past decade, this has become a major focus in academic journals such as *Leadership Quarterly*, *The Journal of Management Studies* and *The European Management Journal* (Ladkin and Taylor 2010). Authentic leadership research is primarily formative, and the concept is still being defined (Caza and Jackson 2011; Northouse 2010). The development of the theory arose from the shortcomings of transformational leadership with respect to ethics. The ethical basis for transformational leadership has been questioned by many researchers, since it is recognised that a leader may manipulate followers in order to attain their goals. For example, Howell and Avolio (1992) provided empirical evidence which supported the contentious assumption that transformational leaders do not need to be ethical. Although Bass and Steidlmeier (2004) responded to this criticism by differentiating between authentic and pseudo-transformational leaders, authentic leadership theory stresses the role of ethics and integrity from the onset of leadership (Caza and Jackson 2011). There is a growing interest in authentic leadership by practitioners and researchers alike (e.g. Avolio and Gardner 2005; Eagly 2005; Gardner and Schermerhorn Jr 2004; Ilies et al. 2005; Ladkin and Taylor 2010; May et al. 2003; Sparrowe 2005; Walumbwa et al. 2008; Yammarino et al. 2008). While there is no single acceptable definition of authentic leadership (Northouse 2010), certain elements are shared by researchers as essential attributes of authentic leaders, namely, self-knowledge, clarity of their values and enacting their roles based on their values and convictions (Shamir and Eilam 2005).

Luthans and Avolio (2003, p. 243) defined authentic leadership as '…a process that draws from both positive psychological capacities and a highly developed organizational context which results in both greater self-awareness and self-regulated positive behaviours on the part of leaders and associates, fostering positive self-development'. This is generally regarded as the starting point of the research into this domain. However, there have been arguments against the inclusion of a moral dimension in authentic leadership (Shamir and Eilam 2005).

The concept of authentic leaders being self-aware of their abilities (proposed by George 2003) and still behaving in an inconsistent manner has been criticised by some researchers (e.g. Kernis 2003). Eagly (2005) suggests that for authenticity to produce positive outcomes, it must be acknowledged by followers; hence, authentic leadership is two-dimensional and relational. Despite the growing interest in and theories proposed by scholars on authentic leadership, there exists little underpinning empirical evidence.

Case Study 3.7

Authentic Leadership

In 2012, many banks were caught up in the LIBOR scandal. LIBOR means the London inter-bank offered rate. It refers to a series of daily interest rate benchmarks administered by the British Bankers' Association (BBA) (H.M. Treasury 2012). It estimates the rate which the banks lend to each other. The rate is based on borrowing costs incurred across more than ten currencies.

There was an alleged attempt by banks to manipulate the LIBOR rates. Banks did this to provide a false perception of their financial health. One of such banks was Barclays. Several emails linking Barclays to the LIBOR scandal are available in the public domain. One of such emails by a trader showing appreciation of the rigged rate states 'Dude I owe you big time! Come over one day after work and I'm opening a bottle of Bollinger!' (Fortune 2012).

Although Barclays was not the worst offender, their case was arguably more prominent due to their charismatic former Chief Executive Officer (CEO) Bob Diamond. Bob Diamond joined Barclays in 1996. He had previously worked for Credit Suisse First Boston and Morgan Stanley International. In 2002, he was appointed the head of asset BGI and by 2010 had risen to the position of Chief Executive Officer (CEO) of Barclays Capital. During his period in Barclays, Diamond had become the crowned jewel of the banking industry. He transformed Barclays and catapulted them into the top tier of global investment banks. One of his notable achievements was his successful and profit-able acquisition of Lehman Brothers in September 2018 for a meagre sum of £1.75 billion.

Many would agree that the fall of Bob Diamond was due to his accumulation of wealth that caught the public eye. There was great controversy about the amount of money he earned. This elicited strong views from people like Lord Mandelson who described him as the 'unacceptable face of banking' (BBC 2012). In 2011, Diamond earned £20.9 million while his actual salary was £250,000. Most of his extra income was due to bonus payments, which many people condemned.

Therefore, it was no surprise that Mr Diamond was not spared with the aftermath of the LIBOR scandal. There were widespread calls for his resignation especially after a telephone conversation emerged between him and Paul Tucker, who was at that time the deputy governor of the Bank of England. The telephone conversation suggested that the Bank of England was in support of the rigging of the LIBOR rate. This led to the resignation of the Chief Operating Officer Jerry del Missier, who was involved in rigging the rate based on this assumption. Mr del Missier was not the only casualty, the Chairman of Barclays, Marcus Agius also resigned and took responsibility for the £453 million settlement in the LIBOR manipulation probe. This is reflected in his statement below

> Last week's events, evidencing as they do unacceptable standards of behaviour within the bank, have dealt a devastating blow to Barclays' reputation. (Financial News 2012)

In a bid to salvage the reputation of Barclays, Diamond finally resigned in July 2012. Though in 2017, the LIBOR scandal still haunts Barclays. Britain's second largest bank is still dealing with investigations into employees' manipulation of LIBOR benchmark interest rates. Jes Stanley, the current CEO has much to do in improving the reputation of Barclays in the Banking Industry. His latest involvement in a whistle-blowing scandal has not helped his credibility. Nevertheless, the board believes that he is the right person to take the organisation ahead.

Questions

- How would you describe the authenticity of Bob Diamond's leadership?
- What are the drawbacks of Diamond's leadership approach?
- How important is authenticity for Jes Stanley in improving the reputation of Barclays?

Entrepreneurial Leadership Theory

Entrepreneurial leadership is a new paradigm that has emerged from the domains of leadership and entrepreneurship. Leadership and entrepreneurship are concepts that have been difficult to define (Bygrave and Hofer 1991; Stogdill 1974). Entrepreneurial leadership, which developed from a convergence of both fields (Fernald et al. 2005), lacks definitional consensus.

There are many definitions of entrepreneurial leadership. It has been defined as a type of leadership that creates visionary scenarios, which in turn are used to assemble and mobilise a 'supporting cast' of participants who become committed to the discovery and exploitation of strategic value creation (Gupta et al. 2004, p. 242). Some scholars (Hejazi et al. 2012; Renko et al. 2015) have stressed the importance of recognising and exploiting opportunities, while others (Greenberg et al. 2013; Surie and Ashley 2008) emphasise the role of entrepreneurial leadership in solving complex problems in uncertain environments. But even with a number of definitions and heightened interest in entrepreneurial leadership, progress has been hindered by the lack of conceptual development and the absence of adequate tools to assess a leader's entrepreneurial characteristics and behaviours (Renko et al. 2015).

Entrepreneurial leadership is a type of leadership capable of identifying and exploiting opportunities in an entrepreneurial environment. Entrepreneurial leaders understand specific functional areas in their business. This understanding spans beyond their business to include situations of varying degrees of complexity. They generate ideas and question assumptions. These individuals understand their own behaviour as well as those of others, and hence are able to develop their abilities and those of their followers. They prioritise their work and manage risks and are successful due to their ability to foster innovation.

This type of leadership has found merit by scholars and practitioners due to the dynamic nature of the business environment and the challenges faced by entrepreneurs and owner managers. As a result, this approach to leadership is worthy of closer scrutiny, and the various conceptions of entrepreneurial leadership are discussed in the next section.

Conceptions of Entrepreneurial Leadership

Eight main approaches for researching the concept of entrepreneurial leadership were uncovered by Harrison (2016) each of which examines the phenomenon from a different perspective. These are as follows:

- Entrepreneurial leadership as a convergence of entrepreneurship and leadership
- The psychological and behavioural profile of entrepreneurial leaders
- The context of entrepreneurial leadership
- Theoretical approaches to entrepreneurial leadership
- Entrepreneurial leadership compared with other forms of leadership
- Entrepreneurial leadership and values
- Entrepreneurial leadership education
- Entrepreneurial leadership and venture performance

The eight conceptual approaches are described in the following subsections:

A Convergence of Entrepreneurship and Leadership

Entrepreneurial leadership has been considered as a convergence of entrepreneurship and leadership (Fernald et al. 2005). Cogliser and Brigham (2004), in a comparative review of the fields of leadership and entrepreneurship, acknowledge that both fields overlap in the areas of vision, influence, innovation and creativity, and planning. However, in their publication, they neither define the concept of entrepreneurial leadership (Roomi and Harrison 2011) nor demonstrate how it can be effectively measured (Gupta et al. 2004; Renko et al. 2015). Essentially, they only provide thoughts on how the field of entrepreneurship can avoid the 'pit falls' (Cogliser and Brigham 2004, p. 771) that exist in the field of leadership. In a review of 136 papers in the fields of entrepreneurship and leadership, Fernald et al. (2005) identified eight characteristics common to both successful entrepreneurs and leaders: the ability to motivate, achievement orientation, creativity, flexibility, patience, persistence, risk-taking and vision. However, their approach to entrepreneurial leadership is descriptive and lacking in analysis and explanation (Roomi and Harrison 2011). They do not suggest how to utilise these common characteristics, and why entrepreneurial leaders possess them. Moreover, entrepreneurial leadership in developing economies is not considered.

Psychological and Behavioural Profile of Entrepreneurial Leaders

Most research done in the field of entrepreneurial leadership to date has sought to identify characteristics deemed to be essential in entrepreneurial leaders (e.g. Darling and Beebe 2007; Gupta et al. 2004; Karanian 2007; Nicholson 1998; Nieuwenhuizen 2009; Renko et al. 2015). According to Karanian (2007), every entrepreneurial leader should possess five core attributes: connection, vivid imagination, family and cultural background, an expectation for confrontation, and a unique gift of character. Communication skills such as paradoxical thinking, controlled reflecting, intentional focusing, instinctive responding, inclusive behaving, purposeful trusting and relational being are put forward by Darling and Beebe (2007) as being essential for entrepreneurial leaders. Nieuwenhuizen (2009) identifies ingenuity, leadership and calculated risk-taking as important attributes of an entrepreneur, while Gupta et al. (2004) identified 19 attributes. These approaches mirror the trait perspective in mainstream leadership research and have been heavily criticised for failing to take into account the impact of context.

Rather than examining the attributes of the entrepreneurial leader, some scholars have sought to identify what entrepreneurial leaders actually do (Flamholtz 2011; Strubler and Redekop 2010) and the strategies they adopt (Darling et al. 2007a, b). Entrepreneurial leadership strategies such as meaning through communication, trust through positioning and confidence through respect have been highlighted (Darling et al. 2007a, b). According to Flamholtz (2011), entrepreneurial leadership functions include creating the vision, managing the organisational culture, coordinating operations, overseeing systems development and leading innovation and change. However, these studies also fail to examine the role of context in entrepreneurial leadership.

Context of Entrepreneurial Leadership

Scholars have examined entrepreneurial leadership in a number of settings. It has been examined from the context of family business (Kansikas et al. 2012; Renko et al. 2015), small and medium-sized enterprises (SMEs) (Leitch et al. 2009), research groups in universities (Hansson and Monsted 2008), the public sector (Currie et al. 2008), non-profit organisations (Santora et al. 1999), directors of libraries (Carpenter 2012), indigenous businesses (Harrison et al. 2016a; Mapunda 2007), gender (Galloway et al. 2015; Patterson et al. 2012a, b), human, social and institutional capital (Leitch et al. 2012), and the aircraft industry (D'Intino et al. 2008).

Other studies have tried to address entrepreneurial leadership from a national (country-based) perspective (Bremer 2009; Choi 2009; Wang et al. 2012) and in terms of its impact in politics (Van Assche 2005). Bremer (2009) compared entrepreneurial leadership in Sweden and China, taking into consideration their political and economic histories, leadership styles and regulations. Wang et al. (2012) examined entrepreneurial leadership from the context of two Chinese firms.

Few scholars have emphasised the context in which this type of leadership is required (Chen 2007; Harrison et al. 2016a; Swiercz and Lydon 2002). Although Chen (2007) appreciates the impact of context, a strategic construct of firms (which are risk-taking, proactiveness and innovation) was used to explain entrepreneurial leadership. However, there remains an ongoing battle among researchers as to whether those dimensions can be used for individual analysis (Renko et al. 2015). Additionally, Swiercz and Lydon (2002) investigated high-tech firms to determine whether organisations undergo transition and to identify the leadership competencies required by successful career entrepreneurial leaders. However, they fail to clearly illustrate how these competencies can be developed, or how training programmes can be established to meet the changes that both the organisation and the entrepreneur face.

These scholars have failed to address entrepreneurial leadership from the dual perspective of leader and follower. Hejazi et al. (2012) have developed and validated a scale for measuring entrepreneurial leadership. However, Hejazi et al. (2012) provide a self-assessment tool, and they only explore entrepreneurial leadership from one perspective and ignore the impact of the follower.

Theoretical Approach to Entrepreneurial Leadership

Most studies on entrepreneurial leadership have taken a theoretical approach rather than an empirical approach (e.g. Ahmed and Ramzan 2013; Greenberg et al. 2013; Harrison et al. 2016b; Hentschke 2010; Kempster and Cope 2010; Kuratko and Hornsby 1999; Kuratko 2007; Patterson et al. 2012b; Van Zyl and Mathur-Helm 2007; Vecchio 2003). For example, Harrison et al. (2016b) provided a systematic literature review of the entrepreneurial leadership paradigm; Kempster and Cope (2010) examined entrepreneurial leadership as a social process; Kuratko and Hornsby (1999) developed a framework for entrepreneurial leadership in corporations; and Kuratko (2007) examined the concept of entrepreneurial leadership by tracing how the theory of entrepreneurship has emerged. Although such studies are significant contributions, they are conceptual and lack an empirical underpinning.

Entrepreneurial Leadership Compared with Other Forms of Leadership

Researchers have also compared entrepreneurial leadership with other forms of leadership (Darling et al. 2007a; Jones and Crompton 2009). Entrepreneurial leadership has been investigated on the basis of enterprise logic and authentic leadership (Jones and Crompton 2009), and charismatic and transformational leadership (Darling et al. 2007a). Although these researchers have found some similarities between entrepreneurial leadership and authentic, charismatic and transformational approaches, they have not produced convincing conceptual frameworks.

Entrepreneurial Leadership and Values

The importance of values in entrepreneurial leadership has been investigated by Darling et al. (2007a, b) and Surie and Ashley (2008). Key leadership values such as joy, charity, hope and peace have been suggested as important in entrepreneurial leadership. Surie and Ashley (2008) went further to develop a framework to show how ethics can be embedded in entrepreneurial leadership by viewing it through the lens of pragmatism. Their findings suggest that following ethical standards may be costly to a new business in the short term.

Entrepreneurial Leadership Education

The value of entrepreneurial leadership education has been investigated by various researchers (e.g. Bagheri and Pihie 2010; Bagheri and Pihie 2011; Okudan and Rzasa 2006; Roomi and Harrison 2011). Entrepreneurial leadership courses have been shown to improve entrepreneurial behaviour among students (Okudan and Rzasa 2006). Research has also been carried out to identify the challenges and competencies of leading university entrepreneurship programmes (Bagheri and Pihie 2011) as well as entrepreneurial leadership learning (Bagheri and Pihie 2010; Roomi and Harrison 2011). However, such work neglects the role of context in shaping entrepreneurial leadership. The impact of culture and demographics in entrepreneurial leadership education has not been considered.

Entrepreneurial Leadership and Venture Performance

The upsurge of interest in entrepreneurial leadership can be attributed at least in part to the assertion by some scholars that it is important for improved performance and organisational success. Sundararajan et al. (2012) suggested that a spiritual entrepreneurial leadership model helps to address the problem of the high rate of start-up failures, although their meditative stance is yet to be tested empirically. Studies have also shown that entrepreneurial leadership has a positive and direct effect on sales performance and customer satisfaction (Agus and Hassan 2010), employee satisfaction, motivation, commitment and effectiveness (Papalexandris and Galanaki 2009). However, these studies (e.g. Hmieleski and Ensley 2007) do not recognise the importance of other dimensions such as opportunity recognition, exploitation or strategising, which may be important to entrepreneurial leadership (Carpenter 2012; Gupta et al. 2004).

Case Study 3.8

Entrepreneurial Leadership

Frank is the newly appointed Chief Operating Officer (COO) of Juice Ltd, an established soft drinks manufacturer based in the UK. It has been in operation since 1947 and has grown from a small local family firm to a national supplier of soft drinks. It has a reputation as an ethical organisation, in relation to its supply chain, employment practices and marketing. Juice Ltd benefits from a diverse employee base, with a range of skills and capabilities. However, some of the senior management have been with the organisation for the majority of their careers and have been promoted through the ranks.

On his appointment, Frank was advised that the organisation was suffering from both a decrease in market share and falling sales. The board of directors has tasked Frank with turning this around, with some limitations. Juice Ltd is keen to retain its brand image as a traditional soft drinks manufacturer and therefore wants to keep its current product portfolio of natural fruit juices. The board is also keen not to make any changes which would challenge its image as an ethical organisation. However, the board does recognise a need for substantial change in order to develop both sustainability and competitive advantage.

Frank's vision for the organisation is to diversify its product range to meet current consumer trends and demand. He is aware of the current focus on health and well-being, and believes this provides significant opportunities for Juice Ltd. His plan is to maintain the current product range, while developing new products such as bottled water and smoothies. However, Frank considers his initial challenge will be changing the mindset of senior management who do not believe this to be fitting with the 'traditional' brand image. This is a key challenge for Frank as senior management hold significant influence over the skilled and enthusiastic employees within their respective departments.

The skilled employees are important to Frank's plans for change. He believes they are a critical factor in creating this change and could assist in winning over the senior management. Frank has created a kaizen team from the existing departments, which is tasked with developing the new organisational direction. While the team is for the most part enthusiastic and motivated, Frank is also concerned that some are caught between the tension of static senior management and this new secondment. There is also the concern that some are getting carried away with this new-found freedom in their roles. Therefore, Frank is faced with the challenge of balancing innovation with the brief and reinvigorating the company while retaining identity.

Questions

- What entrepreneurial leadership attributes does Frank require when presenting his new vision to the senior management and board of directors?
- How can Frank address the tensions experienced by employees in the kaizen team?
- Is Frank an entrepreneurial leader? If so justify?

* This is a fictional case. Names, characters, places and incidents either are products of the author's imagination or are used fictitiously. Any resemblance to actual persons, living or dead, or actual events is purely coincidental.

Summary

In this chapter, the contemporary approaches to leadership, including charismatic, transactional, transformational, distributed, authentic, leader–member exchange, servant and implicit leadership theories, were discussed.

Based on the literature review findings, it could be argued that existing theories do not effectively explain leadership in entrepreneurial settings (see Table 3.1 below, in which the strengths and weaknesses of previous approaches are listed). Entrepreneurial settings are characterised by turbulence, dynamism and change. In a fast-moving business environment, leadership that is capable of identifying and exploiting opportunities is paramount, and hence, entrepreneurial leadership is required.

In this age of globalisation and increased competition, there is a need for business owners to use the most effective leadership approach. In light of the challenges facing entrepreneurs, sound leadership practises are no longer optional but are essential for organisational success.

This chapter has established that leadership is an underdeveloped phenomenon, for which no unified theory currently exists. Leadership studies have traditionally focused narrowly on a limited set of elements by highlighting the leader while overlooking relevant elements of

Table 3.1 Strengths and weaknesses of some of the theories of leadership

Leadership approaches	Strengths	Weaknesses
Great Man/Trait theories	Intuitively appealing and highlights the importance of a leader	Traits are not effective in every situation. It does not explain the role of leadership in ensuring business and organisational coherence
Skill theory	Focuses on leadership skills and competencies	Essentially trait driven and difficult to differentiate skills from traits
Behavioural theory	Identifies leadership behaviour as a core part of the leadership process	Just like trait approach, it fails to consider the situational contingencies associated with leadership
Contingency theory	It emphasises the importance of situations in leadership behaviour	It does not explain why people with certain leadership styles are more effective in particular situations than others
Implicit Leadership theories	Stresses the importance of the social construction of leadership by the followers.	Followers may view such ineffective leadership behaviours as effective. Perception may vary with cultural values and even gender
Leader–member exchange theory	It provides a broader picture of leadership as an interactive exchange process between leaders and followers	It neglects the impact of conflict in the effectiveness of an organisation when followers are grouped into in-groups and out-groups
Servant leadership theory	Views leaders as self-less individuals emphasising the importance of service, which is intuitively appealing	Not suitable for dynamic environments. It does not explain how leaders cope with drastic measures such as organisational change

(continued)

Table 3.1 (continued)

Leadership approaches	Strengths	Weaknesses
Transactional leadership theory	It provides a vivid picture of leadership as an exchange process with the end result the achievement of organisational goals	Focuses mainly on contingent rewards as the tool to influence subordinates. This may not be effective in diverse entrepreneurial settings
Charismatic/ Transformational leadership theories	Conceptualises leadership as valuable in organisations facing turbulence and turmoil	A modification of the trait approach and fails to explain clearly how such characteristics can improve organisational effectiveness
Distributed leadership theory	Emphasises the importance of group effort and participation in leadership	It may not be feasible in every context especially in small businesses where subordinates adulate their leaders and resist empowerment
Authentic leadership theory	Stresses the importance of integrity and ethics in leadership	Fails to explain how authenticity will always produce positive outcomes especially in entrepreneurial settings

leadership (such as the follower and the context) (Avolio 2007; Zaccaro and Klimoski 2001). There remains a need for more research which considers both leaders' and followers' perspectives.

References

Ahmed, A., & Ramzan, M. (2013). A learning and improvement model in entrepreneurial leadership. *IOSR Journal of Business and Management, 11*(6), 50–60.

Agus, A., & Hassan, Z. (2010). The structural influence of entrepreneurial leadership, communication skills, determination and motivation on sales and customer satisfaction. *International Journal of Business and Development Studies, 2*(1), 109–130.

Avolio, B. J., & Gardner, W. L. (2005). Authentic leadership development: Getting to the root of positive forms of leadership. *The Leadership Quarterly, 16*(3), 315–338.

Avolio, B. J. (2007). Promoting more integrative strategies for leadership theory-building. *American Psychologist, 62*(1), 25.

Bagheri, A., & Pihie, Z. A. L. (2010). Entrepreneurial leadership learning: In search of missing links. *Procedia - Social and Behavioral Sciences, 7,* 70–79.

Bagheri, A., & Pihie, Z. A. L. (2011). On becoming an entrepreneurial leader: A focus on the impacts of university entrepreneurship programs. *American Journal of Applied Sciences, 8*(9), 884–892.

Barbuto, J. E., & Wheeler, D. W. (2006). Scale development and construct clarification of servant leadership. *Group and Organization Management, 31*(3), 300–326.

Bass, B. M. (1985). *Leadership and performance beyond expectations.* New York: Free Press.

Bass, B. M., & Avolio, B. J. (1990). *Transformational leadership development: manual for multifactor leadership questionnaire.* California: Palo Alto Consulting Psychologists Press.

Bass, B. M., & Avolio, B. J. (1994). *Improving organizational effectiveness through transformational leadership.* Newbury Park, CA: Sage.

Bass, B. M., & Steidlmeier, P. (2004). Ethics, character, and authentic transformational leadership behavior. In J. B. Ciulla (Ed.), *Ethics, the Heart of Leadership* (pp. 175–196). Preger: Westport Co.

Bausch, T. (1998). Servant-leaders making human new models of work and organization. In L. C. Spears (Ed.), *Insights on leadership: Service, stewardship, spirit, and servant-leadership* (pp. 230–245). New York: Wiley.

BBC (2012). Profile: Barclays' chief executive Bob Diamond. http://www.bbc.co.uk/news/business-18625227. Accessed June 13, 2017.

Bennis, W. G., & Nanus, B. (1985). *Leaders: The strategies for taking charge.* New York: Harper & Row.

Bremer, I. (2009). Common factors between Swedish and Chinese entrepreneurial leadership styles. *Business Intelligence Journal, 2*(1), 9–41.

Bryman, A. (1987). The generalizability of implicit leadership theory. *The Journal of Social Psychology, 127*(2), 129–141.

Burns, J. M. (1978). *Leadership.* New York: Harper & Row.

Bygrave, W. D., & Hofer, C. W. (1991). Theorizing about entrepreneurship. *Entrepreneurship Theory and Practice, 16*(2), 13–22.

Calder, B. J. (1977). An attribution theory of leadership. In J. Salancik & B. Staw (Eds.), *New directions in organizational behaviour* (pp. 47–62). New York: St. Clair Press.

Carless, S. A. (1998). Assessing the discriminant validity of transformational leader behaviour as measured by the MLQ1. *Journal of Occupational and Organizational Psychology, 71*(4), 353–358.

Carpenter, M. T. H. (2012). Cheerleader, opportunity seeker, and master strategist: ARL directors as entrepreneurial leaders. *College & Research Libraries, 73*(1), 11–32.

Caza, A., & Jackson, B. (2011). Authentic leadership. In A. Bryman, D. Collinson, K. Grint, B. Jackson, & M. Uhl-Bien (Eds.), *The sage handbook of leadership* (pp. 352–364). London: Sage.

Chen, M. (2007). Entrepreneurial leadership & new ventures: Creativity in entrepreneurial teams. *Creativity & Innovation Management, 16*(3), 239–249.

Choi, E. K. (2009). Entrepreneurial leadership in the Meiji cotton spinners' early conceptualisation of global competition. *Business History, 51*(6), 927–958.

Cogliser, C. C., & Brigham, K. H. (2004). The intersection of leadership and entrepreneurship: Mutual lessons to be learned. *The Leadership Quarterly, 15*(6), 771–799.

Conger, J. A. (2011). Charismatic leadership. In A. Bryman, D. Collinson, K. Grint, B. Jackson, & M. Uhl-Bien (Eds.), *The sage handbook of leadership* (pp. 86–102). London: Sage.

Conger, J. A., & Kanungo, R. N. (1987). Toward a behavioral theory of charismatic leadership in organizational settings. *The Academy of Management Review, 12*(4), 637–647.

Conger, J. A., & Kanungo, R. N. (1998). *Charismatic leadership in organizations.* Thousand Oaks: Sage.

Cope, J., Kempster, S., & Parry, K. (2011). Exploring distributed leadership in the small business context. *International Journal of Management Reviews, 13*(3), 270–285.

Currie, G., Humphreys, M., Ucbasaran, D., & Mcmanus, S. (2008). Entrepreneurial leadership in the English public sector: Paradox or possibility? *Public Administration, 86*(4), 987–1008.

Daft, R. L. (1999). *Leadership Theory and Practice.* Orlando: The Dryden Press, Harcourt Brace College Publishers.

Dansereau, F., Jr., Graen, G. & Haga, W. J. (1975). A vertical dyad linkage approach to leadership within formal organizations: A longitudinal investigation of the role making process. *Organizational Behavior and Human Performance, 13*(1), 46–78.

Darling, J. R., & Beebe, S. A. (2007). Enhancing entrepreneurial leadership: A focus on key communication priorities. *Journal of Small Business & Entrepreneurship, 20*(2), 151–167.

Darling, J. R., Gabrielsson, M., & Seristö, H. (2007a). Enhancing contemporary entrepreneurship: A focus on management leadership. *European Business Review, 19*(1), 4–22.

Darling, J. R., Keeffe, M. J., & Ross, J. K. (2007b). Entrepreneurial leadership strategies and values: Keys to operational excellence. *Journal of Small Business & Entrepreneurship, 20*(1), 41–54.

Diaz-Saenz, H. R. (2011). Transformational leadership. In A. Bryman, D. Collinson, K. Grint, B. Jackson, & M. Uhl-Bien (Eds.), *The sage handbook of leadership* (pp. 299–310). London: Sage.

D'Intino, R. S., Boyles, T., Neck, C. P., & Hall, J. R. (2008). Visionary entrepreneurial leadership in the aircraft industry: The Boeing Company legacy. *Journal of Management History, 14*(1), 39–54.

Dionne, S. D., Yammarino, F. J., Atwater, L. E., & Spangler, W. D. (2004). Transformational leadership and team performance. *Journal of Organizational Change Management, 17*(2), 177–193.

Eagly, A. H. (2005). Achieving relational authenticity in leadership: Does gender matter? *The Leadership Quarterly, 16*(3), 459–474.

Ensley, M. D., Hmieleski, K. M., & Pearce, C. L. (2006). The importance of vertical and shared leadership within new venture top management teams: Implications for the performance of startups. *The Leadership Quarterly, 17*(3), 217–231.

Fernald, L. W., Jr., Solomon, G. T., & Tarabishy, A. (2005). A new paradigm: Entrepreneurial leadership. *Southern Business Review, 30*(2), 1–10.

Financial News. (2012). Barclays' chairman Agius resigns. https://www.fnlondon.com/articles/barclays-agius-is-stepping-down-20120702. Accessed June 13, 2017.

Flamholtz, E. G. (2011). The leadership molecule hypothesis: Implications for entrepreneurial organizations. *International Review of Entrepreneurship, 9*(3), 1–23.

Forbes. (2012). Jeff Bezos's top 10 leadership lessons. https://www.forbes.com/sites/georgeanders/2012/04/04/bezos-tips/#3870d822fce4. Accessed May 22, 2017.

Fortune. (2012). The death of Bob Diamond's Dream for Barclays. http://fortune.com/2012/07/30/the-death-of-bob-diamonds-dream-for-barclays/?iid=sr-link1. Accessed June 13, 2017.

Galloway, L., Kapasi, I., & Sang, K. (2015). Entrepreneurship, leadership, and the value of feminist approaches to understanding them. *Journal of Small Business Management, 53*(3), 683–692.

Gardner, W. L., & Schermerhorn, J. R., Jr. (2004). Unleashing individual potential: Performance gains through positive organizational behavior and authentic leadership. *Organizational Dynamics, 33*(3), 270–281.

Gavan O'Shea, P., Foti, R. J., Hauenstein, N. M. A., & Bycio, P. (2009). Are the best leaders both transformational and transactional? A pattern-oriented analysis. *Leadership, 5*(2), 237–259.

George, B. (2003). *Authentic leadership: Rediscovering the secrets of creating lasting value.* San Francisco: Jossey-Bass.

Gill, R. (2011). *Theory and practice of leadership* (2nd ed.). London: Sage.

Gladwell, M. (2011). The tweaker: The real genius of Steve Jobs. http://www.newyorker.com/magazine/2011/11/14/the-tweaker. Accessed May 22, 2017.

Graen, G. B., & Cashman, J. F. (1975). A role-making model of leadership in formal organisations: a developmental approach. In J. G. Hunt & L. L. Larson (Eds.), *Leadership Frontiers* (pp. 143–165). Kent: Kent State University Press.

Graen, G. B., & Uhl-Bien, M. (1995). Relationship-based approach to leadership: Development of leader-member exchange (LMX) theory of leadership over 25 years: Applying a multi-level multi-domain perspective. *The Leadership Quarterly, 6*(2), 219–247.

Greenberg, D., McKone-Sweet, K. & Wilson, H. J. (2013). Entrepreneurial leaders: Creating opportunity in an unknowable world. *Leader to Leader, 2013*(67), 56–62.

Greenleaf, R. K. (1977). *Servant leadership: A journey into the nature of legitimate power and greatness.* Mahwah, New Jersey: Paulist Press.

Greenleaf, R. K. (1998). Servant–leadership. In L. C. Spears (Ed.), *Insights on Leadership* (pp. 15–20). New York: Wiley.

Gronn, P. (2002). Distributed leadership as a unit of analysis. *The Leadership Quarterly, 13*(4), 423–451.

Gupta, V., Macmillan, I. C., & Surie, G. (2004). Entrepreneurial leadership: developing and measuring a cross-cultural construct. *Journal of Business Venturing, 19*(2), 241–260.

Hansson, F., & Mønsted, M. (2008). Research leadership as entrepreneurial organizing for research. *Higher Education, 55*(6), 651–670.

Harris, A. (2004). Distributed leadership and school improvement: Leading or misleading? *Educational Management Administration & Leadership, 32*(1), 11–24.

Harrison, C. (2016). *Entrepreneurial Leadership in a Developing Economy: A Study in Nigeria (Doctoral Thesis)*. Scotland: University of the West of Scotland.

Harrison, C., Paul, S., & Burnard, K. (2016a). Entrepreneurial leadership in retail pharmacy: developing economy perspective. *Journal of Workplace Learning, 28*(3), 150–167.

Harrison, C., Paul, S., & Burnard, K. (2016b). Entrepreneurial leadership in retail pharmacy: A systematic literature review. *International Review of Entrepreneurship, 14*(2), 235–264.

Hejazi, A. M., Maleki, M. M., & Naeji, M. J. (2012). Designing a scale for measuring entrepreneurial leadership in SME's. *International Proceedings of Economics Development and Research, 28*(1), 71–77.

Hentschke, G. C. (2010). Developing entrepreneurial leaders. In B. Davies & M. Brundrett (Eds.), *Developing Successful Leadership* (pp. 115–132). Netherlands: Springer.

Hmieleski, K. M., & Ensley, M. D. (2007). A contextual examination of new venture performance: entrepreneur leadership behavior, top management team heterogeneity, and environmental dynamism. *Journal of Organizational Behavior, 28*(7), 865–889.

H.M. Treasury. (2012). *The Wheatley Review of Libor: Final Report*. London: H.M. Treasury.

House, R. J. (1977). A 1976 theory of charismatic leadership. In J. G. Hunt & L. L. Larson (Eds.), *Leadership: The cutting edge* (pp. 189–207). Carbondale, Illinois: Southern Illinois University Press.

House, R. J., & Aditya, R. N. (1997). The social scientific study of leadership: Quo vadis? *Journal of Management, 23*(3), 409–473.

Howell, J. M., & Avolio, B. J. (1992). The ethics of charismatic leadership: submission or liberation? *Academy of Management Executive, 6*(2), 43–54.

Ilies, R., Morgeson, F. P., & Nahrgang, J. D. (2005). Authentic leadership and eudaemonic well-being: Understanding leader–follower outcomes. *The Leadership Quarterly, 16*(3), 373–394.

Issacson, W. (2011). *Steve jobs*. U.S: Simon & Schuster.

Jones, O., & Crompton, H. (2009). Enterprise logic and small firms: A model of authentic entrepreneurial leadership. *Journal of Strategy and Management, 2*(4), 329–351.

Judge, T. A., & Piccolo, R. F. (2004). Transformational and transactional leadership: A meta-analytic test of their relative validity. *Journal of Applied Psychology, 89*(5), 755–767.

Kansikas, J., Laakkonen, A., Sarpo, V., & Kontinen, T. (2012). Entrepreneurial leadership and familiness as resources for strategic entrepreneurship. *International Journal of Entrepreneurial Behaviour & Research, 18*(2), 141–158.

Karanian, B. (2007). Entrepreneurial leadership: A balancing act in engineering and science. *American Society for Engineering Education (ASEE), AC 2007–2804: Entrepreneurial Leadership and Transformational Change Global Colloquia*, Rio de Janeiro, Brazil.

Kempster, S., & Cope, J. (2010). Learning to lead in the entrepreneurial context. *International Journal of Entrepreneurial Behaviour & Research, 16*(1), 5–34.

Kernis, M. H. (2003). Toward a conceptualization of optimal self-esteem. *Psychological Inquiry, 14*(1), 1–26.

Kouzes, J. M., & Posner, B. Z. (1987). *The leadership challenge: How to get extraordinary things done in organizations*. San Francisco: Jossey-Bass.

Kouzes, J. M., & Posner, B. Z. (2002). *The Leadership Challenge* (3rd ed.). San Francisco: Jossey-Bass.

Kuratko, D. F., & Hornsby, J. S. (1999). Corporate entrepreneurial leadership for the 21st century. *Journal of Leadership & Organizational Studies, 5*(2), 27–39.

Kuratko, D. F. (2007). Entrepreneurial leadership in the 21st century. *Journal of Leadership & Organizational Studies, 13*(4), 1–11.

Ladkin, D., & Taylor, S. S. (2010). Enacting the 'true self': Towards a theory of embodied authentic leadership. *The Leadership Quarterly, 21*(1), 64–74.

Laub, J. A., Braye, R. H., Horsman, J. H., Beazley, D. A., Thompson, R. S., Ledbetter, D. S., et al. (1999). *Assessing the servant organization: Development of the servant organizational leadership assessment (sola) instrument*. Florida: Florida Atlantic University Press.

Leitch, C. M., McMullan, C., & Harrison, R. T. (2009). Leadership development in SMEs: An action learning approach. *Action Learning: Research and Practice, 6*(3), 243–263.

Leitch, C. M., McMullan, C., & Harrison, R. T. (2012). The development of entrepreneurial leadership: The role of human, social and institutional capital. *British Journal of Management, 24*(3), 347–366.

Liden, R. C., & Maslyn, J. M. (1998). Multidimensionality of leader-member exchange: An empirical assessment through scale development. *Journal of Management, 24*(1), 43–72.

Liden, R. C., Wayne, S. J., Zhao, H., & Henderson, D. (2008). Servant leadership: Development of a multidimensional measure and multi-level assessment. *The Leadership Quarterly, 19*(2), 161–177.

Lord, R. G., Foti, R., & Phillips, J. S. (1982). A theory of leadership categorization. In J. G. Hunt, U. Sekaran, & C. A. Schriesheim (Eds.), *leadership* (pp. 104–121). Beyond Establishment Views, Carbondale, Illinios: Southern Illinois University Press.

Lord, R. G., Foti, R. J., & DeVader, C. L. (1984). A test of leadership categorization theory: Internal structure, information processing, and leadership perceptions. *Organizational Behavior and Human Performance, 34*(3), 343–378.

Lord, R. D., & Maher, K. J. (1991). *Leadership and Information Processing: Linking Perceptions and Performance.* Boston: Unwind Hyman.

Lord, R. C., & Maher, K. J. (1993). *Leadership and information processing: Linking perceptions and performance.* London: Routledge.

Lowe, K. B., Kroeck, K. G., & Sivasubramaniam, N. (1996). Effectiveness correlates of transformational and transactional leadership: A meta-analytic review of the literature. *The Leadership Quarterly, 7*(3), 385–425.

Lussier, R. N., & Achua, C. F. (2001). *Leadership: Theory, Application & Skill Development.* Ohio: South Western College Publishing, Thomson learning.

Luthans, F., & Avolio, B. (2003). Authentic leadership: A positive development approach. In K. S. Cameron, J. E. Dutton, & R. E. Quinn (Eds.), *Positive organizational scholarship* (pp. 241–258). Berrett-Koehler: San Francisco, California.

Mapunda, G. (2007). Entrepreneurial leadership and indigenous enterprise development. *Journal of Asia Entrepreneurship and Sustainability, 3*(3), 1–16.

May, D. R., Chan, A. Y. L., Hodges, T. D., & Avolio, B. J. (2003). Developing the moral component of authentic leadership. *Organizational Dynamics, 32*(3), 247–260.

Mehra, A., Smith, B. R., Dixon, A. L., & Robertson, B. (2006). Distributed leadership in teams: The network of leadership perceptions and team performance. *The Leadership Quarterly, 17*(3), 232–245.

Meindl, J. R., Ehrlich, S. B., & Dukerich, J. M. (1985). The romance of leadership. *Administrative Science Quarterly, 30*(1), 78–102.

Nicholson, N. (1998). Personality & entrepreneurial leadership: A style of the heads of the UK's most successful companies. *European Management Journal, 16*(5), 529–539.

Nieuwenhuizen, C. (2009). Entrepreneurial leadership and management for change and successful business growth, [Online]. Paper presented at

2nd International UJ Faculty of Management Conference, Johannesburg, University of Johannesburg, 11–13 March 2009, http://hdl.handle.net/10210/5267. Accessed September 9, 2013.

Northouse, P. G. (2010). *Leadership: Theory and Practice* (5th ed.). California: Sage.

Okudan, G. E., & Rzasa, S. E. (2006). A project-based approach to entrepreneurial leadership education. *Technovation, 26*(2), 195–210.

Page, D. & Wong, T. P. (2000). *A conceptual framework for measuring servant-leadership. The human factor in shaping the course of history and development.* Lanham, MD: University Press of America.

Papalexandris, N., & Galanaki, E. (2009). Leadership's impact on employee engagement: Differences among entrepreneurs and professional CEOs. *Leadership & Organization Development Journal, 30*(4), 365–385.

Patterson, N., Mavin, S., & Turner, J. (2012a). Unsettling the gender binary: experiences of gender in entrepreneurial leadership and implications for HRD. *European Journal of Training and Development, 36*(7), 687–711.

Patterson, N., Mavin, S., & Turner, J. (2012b). Envisioning female entrepreneur: leaders anew from a gender perspective. *Gender in Management: An International Journal, 27*(6), 395–416.

Pearce, C. L., & Sims, H. P. (2002). Vertical versus shared leadership as predictors of the effectiveness of change management teams: An examination of aversive, directive, transactional, transformational, and empowering leader behaviors. *Group Dynamics, 6*(2), 172–197.

Phillips, J. S., & Lord, R. G. (1981). Causal attributions and perceptions of leadership. *Organizational Behavior and Human Performance, 28*(2), 143–163.

Podsakoff, P. M., Mackenzie, S. B., Moorman, R. H., & Fetter, R. (1990). Transformational leader behaviors and their effects on followers' trust in leader, satisfaction, and organizational citizenship behaviors. *The Leadership Quarterly, 1*(2), 107–142.

Renko, M., Tarabishy, A., Carsrud, A. L., & Brannback, M. (2015). Understanding & measuring entrepreneurial leadership. *Journal of Small Business Management, 53*(1), 54–74.

Roomi, M. A., & Harrison, P. (2011). Entrepreneurial leadership: What is it & how should it be taught? *International Review of Entrepreneurship, 9*(3), 1–44.

Russell, R. F., & Stone, A. G. (2002). A review of servant leadership attributes: Developing a practical model. *Leadership & Organization Development Journal, 23*(3), 145–157.

Santora, J. C., Seaton, W., & Sarros, J. C. (1999). Changing times: Entrepreneurial leadership in a community-based non-profit organization. *Journal of Leadership & Organizational Studies, 6*(3–4), 101–109.

Scandura, T. A. (1999). Rethinking leader-member exchange: An organizational justice perspective. *The Leadership Quarterly, 10*(1), 25–40.

Sendjaya, S., & Sarros, J. C. (2002). Servant leadership: Its origin, development, and application in organizations. *Journal of Leadership & Organizational Studies, 9*(2), 57–64.

Shamir, B., & Eilam, G. (2005). "What's your story?" A life-stories approach to authentic leadership development. *The Leadership Quarterly, 16*(3), 395–417.

Shamir, B., House, R., J. & Arthur, M. B. (1993). The motivational effects of charismatic leadership: A self-concept based theory. *Organizational Science, 4*(4), 577–594.

Sias, P. M., & Jablin, E. M. (1995). Differential superior-subordinate relations, perception of fairness, and co-worker communication. *Human Communication Research, 22*(1), 5–38.

Smith, B. N., Montagno, R. V., & Kuzmenko, T. N. (2004). Transformational and servant leadership: Content and contextual comparisons. *Journal of Leadership & Organizational Studies, 10*(4), 80–91.

Sparrowe, R. T. (2005). Authentic leadership and the narrative self. *The Leadership Quarterly, 16*(3), 419–439.

Spears, L. C. (1998). Introduction: Tracing the growing impact of servant-leadership. In L. C. Spears (Ed.), *Insights on Leadership: Service, Stewardship, Spirit, and Servant-Leadership* (pp. 1–12). New York: Wiley.

Spillane, J. P. (2005). Distributed leadership. *The Educational Forum, 69*(2), 143–150.

Spillane, J. P., Halverson, R., & Diamond, J. B. (2001). Investigating school leadership practice: A distributed perspective. *Educational Researcher, 30*(3), 23–28.

Stogdill, R. M. (1974). *Handbook of Leadership*. New York: Free Press.

Strubler, D. C., & Redekop, B. W. (2010). Entrepreneurial human resource leadership: A conversation with Dwight Carlson. *Human Resource Management, 49*(4), 793–804.

Sundararajan, M., Sundararajan, B., & Henderson, S. (2012). Role of meditative foundation entrepreneurial leadership and new venture success. *Spirituality, Leadership and Management, 6*(1), 59–70.

Surie, G., & Ashley, A. (2008). Integrating pragmatism and ethics in entrepreneurial leadership for sustainable value creation. *Journal of Business Ethics, 81*(1), 235–246.

Swiercz, P. M., & Lydon, S. R. (2002). Entrepreneurial leadership in high-tech firms: A field study. *Leadership & Organization Development Journal, 23*(7), 380–389.

Van Assche, T. (2005). The impact of entrepreneurial leadership on EU high politics: A case study of Jacques Delors and the creation of EMU. *Leadership, 1*(3), 279–298.

Van Zyl, H., & Mathur-Helm, B. (2007). Exploring a conceptual model, based on the combined effects of entrepreneurial leadership, market orientation and relationship marketing orientation on South Africa's small tourism business performance. *South African Journal of Business Management, 38*(2), 17–24.

Vecchio, R. P. (2003). Entrepreneurship and leadership: common trends and common threads. *Human Resource Management Review, 13*(2), 303–327.

Walumbwa, F. O., Avolio, B. J., Gardner, W. L., Wernsing, T. S., & Peterson, S. J. (2008). Authentic leadership: Development and validation of a theory-based measure. *Journal of Management, 34*(1), 89–126.

Wang, C. L., Tee, D. D., & Ahmed, P. K. (2012). Entrepreneurial leadership and context in Chinese firms: A tale of two Chinese private enterprises. *Asia Pacific Business Review, 18*(4), 505–530.

Weber, M. (1947). *The Theory of Social and Economic Organizations, Translated by T.* Parsons, New York: Free Press.

Wright, P. (1996). *Managerial Leadership.* London: Routledge.

Yammarino, F. J., Spangler, W. D., & Bass, B. M. (1993). Transformational leadership and performance: A longitudinal investigation. *The Leadership Quarterly, 4*(1), 81–102.

Yammarino, F. J., Dionne, S. D., Schriesheim, C. A., & Dansereau, F. (2008). Authentic leadership and positive organizational behavior: A meso, multi-level perspective. *The Leadership Quarterly, 19*(6), 693–707.

Yukl, G. (2010). *Leadership in Organisations, 7*th ed. Upper Saddle River, New Jersey: Pearson Education Limited.

Zaccaro, S. J., & Klimoski, R. J. (2001). The nature of organizational leadership: An introduction. In S. J. Zaccaro & R. J. Klimoski (Eds.), *The nature of organizational leadership: understanding the performance imperatives confronting today's leaders* (pp. 3–41). San Francisco, California: Jossey-Bass.

4

Conclusion

Abstract Therefore, anyone aspiring to leadership should know the skills that effective leaders have and ways in which they may be developed. The book concludes with this chapter on leadership development. The skills required for developing oneself as a leader is identified and discussed. This is supported with empirical evidence and research findings from scholars. Technical skills, conceptual skills and interpersonal skills and their sub-skill set are discussed in detail. With the emphasis on leadership skills in today's world, it has become paramount that all individuals who aspire to be leaders must know how to develop the required skill set. These methods, which include mentoring, leadership training programmes and personal growth activities, are discussed in this chapter.

Keywords Technical skills · Conceptual skills · Interpersonal skills Entrepreneurial skills · Leadership skills development

© The Author(s) 2018
C. Harrison, *Leadership Theory and Research*,
https://doi.org/10.1007/978-3-319-68672-1_4

Introduction

Therefore, anyone aspiring to leadership should know the skills that effective leaders have and ways in which they may be developed. The earlier chapters had focused on the conceptions and theories of leadership. The book concludes with the chapter on leadership development. The skills required for developing oneself as a leader are identified and discussed. This is supported with empirical evidence and research findings from scholars. Technical skills, conceptual skills and interpersonal skills and their sub-skill set are discussed in detail.

With the emphasis on leadership skills in today's world, it has become paramount that all individuals who aspire to be leaders must know how to develop the required skill set. These methods which include mentoring, leadership training programmes and personal growth activities are discussed in this chapter.

The importance of the different skill set may vary depending on the level of management. This is examined in this chapter. These skills have found merit among leadership scholars and are worthy of close scrutiny and are discussed below.

Technical Skills

Technical skill is the in-depth understanding of and the proficiency in a specific type of activity, particularly one involving methods, processes, procedures or techniques (Katz 1974). It includes competencies in a specialised area as well as analytical ability (Katz 1955). This skill includes factual knowledge about the organisation and its products and services. Such knowledge is usually obtained by a combination of training, formal education and job experience (Haq 2011; Yukl 2010). To successfully guide subordinates and steer the organisation to success, an in-depth knowledge of the products and services offered is a prerequisite.

Technical skills have been shown to be an important factor in enhancing a leader's performance (Bass 1990; Haq 2011; Katz 1955; Katz 1974;

Lord and Hall 2005; Shiba 1998). However, research has also shown that technical skills vary at different levels of management (McCall and Lombardo 1983), becoming less relevant at higher levels of management (Bass 1990; McCall and Lombardo 1983; Northouse 2010). Nevertheless, recent research by Mumford et al. (2007) provides contrary evidence, with the inference that higher levels of an organisation require higher levels of all leadership skills. Although no consensus may have been reached on whether technical skills become more or less important as an individual moves up the organisational ladder, there is an agreement among scholars that technical skills are required in every leader. Indeed, it can be argued that technical skills are even more important for an entrepreneur. Research on entrepreneurs who established successful companies suggests that technical knowledge is the fertile ground in which seeds of inspiration yields innovative products (Westley and Mintzberg 1989). In addition, it is not sufficient for entrepreneurs to have extensive technical knowledge of their own products and services; knowledge of their competitors in this respect is also vital (Yukl 2010).

Researchers have classified these skills under subcomponents such as business skills (Mumford et al. 2007; Siewiorek et al. 2012) and technological skills (Zaccaro and Klimoski 2001), or under the broader umbrella term of task skills (Lord and Hall 2005). Leaders of today's organisations are expected to possess business skills, which relate to managing material, human and financial resources (Katz 1974; Luthans et al. 1988; Mumford et al. 2007). The effective management of these resources form the bedrock of any successful business, and any individual who possesses such skills stands a greater chance of succeeding in such a dynamic and turbulent environment.

Human Skills

Human skills involve the knowledge and ability to work with people. These include knowledge about human behaviour and group processes; the ability to understand other people's feelings, attitudes and motives; and the ability to communicate unambiguously and persuasively (Yukl 2010). In addition, human skills, as cited in Mumford et al. (2007,

p. 157), include '…skills required for coordination of actions of one-self and others (Gillen and Carroll 1985; Mumford et al. 2000b), nego-tiation skills for reconciling differences among employee perspectives and establishing mutually satisfying relationships (Copeman 1971; Mahoney et al. 1963; Mahoney et al. 1965; Mintzberg 1973); and, per-suasion skills to influence others to more effectively accomplish organi-zational objectives (Katz 1974; Mintzberg 1973; Yukl 1989)'. It is these skills that help a leader to work effectively with their subordinates to achieve the set objectives of the organisation. In short, human skills are people skills (Northouse 2010), and without such skills, the capacity to get along with other people is almost impossible.

Human skills form the basis for leadership, since leadership is about influencing people. Hence, the focus of possessing such skills cannot be overemphasised. These skills are not limited to just influencing other peo-ple, but also include understanding their perspectives and seeing matters from their points of view. Hence, leaders ought to be empathetic. The human skill perspective, first introduced by Katz (1955), is broad and has since been broken down into several components. Even Katz (1974) introduced social skills in conjunction with human skills, while many other researchers have preferred the term 'interpersonal skills' (Haq 2011; Mumford et al. 2007; Wright and Taylor 1994; Yukl 2010). Under the broad reach of human skills, skills such as empathy (Yukl 2010), self- or meta-monitoring, adjustment of one's behaviour to fit the situation (Lord and Hall 2005) and influence and management tactics (Harris et al. 2007) have been placed. As with technical skills, researchers have shown that human skills are important in management as well as in leadership (Bass 1990; Boyatzis 1982; McCall and Lombardo 1983; Wright and Taylor 1994). However, unlike technical skills, Katz (1955, 1974) sug-gests that human skills are equally important at any level of management.

Conceptual Skills

As the name implies, conceptual skills involve dealing with concepts and ideas. People who possess such skills are comfortable with hypo-thetical notions and abstractions. According to Yukl (2010), conceptual skills include good judgement, foresight, intuition, creativity and the ability to understand ambiguous and uncertain events. The leader who possesses conceptual skills sees the enterprise as a whole and recognises how its various functions depend on one another, and how changes in any part may affect the whole (Schedlitzki and Edwards 2014).

Conceptual skills have been referred to as cognitive skills by a number of scholars such as Katz (1955, 1974) and Mumford et al. (2007). Some researchers use the term 'cognitive abilities' (Mumford et al. 2000a, 2000b, 2000c, 2000d; Zaccaro et al. 2000). Whatever label is used, skills in this area are key to leadership and include proficiency in oral communication (Shipper and Dillard 2000); written communication (Wright 1996); active listening (Graham 1983); active learning (Jacobs and Jaques 1987); critical thinking (Gillen and Carroll 1985); analysing the strengths and weaknesses of approaches taken; and cognitive complexity (Yukl 2010), which refers to the ability to identify complex relations and to provide creative solutions to problems.

Leaders need conceptual skills for effective organisation and planning. To succeed in any organisation, leaders need to understand how its components work, and how changes, especially in the external environment, will affect its competitive position. Strategic skills are conceptual skills that include dealing with ambiguity and exerting an influence in the organisation (Mumford et al. 2007; Siewiorek et al. 2012). These enable leaders to recognise relationships between problems and opportunities, and to implement appropriate strategies to deal with them (Mumford et al. 2007).

Katz proposed that the need for conceptual skills increases as an individual ascends to higher levels of management. Researchers have shown an increased requirement for conceptual skills in higher levels of the organisational hierarchy (Mumford et al. 2007; Pavett and Lau 1983). Indeed, Mumford et al. (2007) showed that strategic skills, which are highly conceptual skills, only fully emerge at the highest levels in an organisation.

Many scholars lament that the conceptualisation of leadership skills has received insufficient attention (e.g. Mumford et al. 2007; Wright 1996; Yammarino 2000). Mumford et al. (2007) have appealed for a greater focus on leadership skills with the argument that leaders can become better leaders. By learning and developing even better leadership skills, an individual will be able to lead more effectively, as well as influence people to accomplish set goals and objectives (Siewiorek et al. 2012). According to Gordon and Yukl (2004, p. 364), 'More research is needed on traits and skills that seem especially relevant for leadership in a complex, turbulent environment (e.g. emotional intelligence, social intelligence, systems thinking, situational awareness, personal integrity)'. In today's volatile and turbulent business environment, the importance of possessing leadership skills cannot be overemphasised.

Other Leadership Skills

Business Skills

Katz's (1974) framework does not dichotomise technical skills into business skills but takes a broader perspective by considering business skills as technical skills. By contrast, studies have identified technical skills and business skills as separate, not similar, entities (Mumford et al. 2007; Siewiorek et al. 2012). Indeed, business skills are critical leadership skills for any organisation. This position is also supported by literature in the domain of entrepreneurial leadership. (Ballein 1998; Guo 2009; Hentschke 2010; Swiercz and Lydon 2002).

The business skills can be developed by training and development programmes. This is important in leadership development (Day 2001; Mumford et al. 2000a; Paul and Whittam 2015), in that well-timed training interventions can promote the development of leadership skills in general.

In particular, the business skills could range from accounting and financial management (Copeman 1971; Hentschke 2010; Zaccaro and Klimoski 2001), administration (Swiercz and Lydon 2002) and managing human resources (Luthans et al. 1988; Mahoney et al. 1965). Nevertheless, all these business skills can be developed formally by training, or informally by independent learning.

Conceptual Skills

Leaders are able to understand situations of varying degrees of complexity. This is similar to the conceptual skill element in Katz's framework on leadership set out earlier. In this section, six forms of conceptual skills are identified as important for effective leadership.

Analytical Skills

Leaders need to be analytical in their decision-making and risk-taking. This is consistent with findings in the literature that effective leaders have the cognitive capacities such as collecting, processing and disseminating information, analytical ability and logical thinking (Mumford et al. 2007; Yukl 2010). Leaders should be able to think objectively. The use of logic to analyse the strengths and weaknesses of different approaches to work is critical for success as a leader (Gillen and Carroll 1985; Mumford et al. 2007).

Idea Generation Skills

The ability to generate new ideas and question assumptions is a vital skill for effective leadership. Leaders especially based on entrepreneurial leadership literature should be innovative and skilled in generating new ideas. These leaders have to be creative and develop new and useful ideas in terms of entrepreneurial opportunity recognition, resource utilisation and problem-solving (Agbim et al. 2013; Bagheri and Pihie 2011; Ballein 1998; Carpenter 2012; Chen 2007; Gupta et al. 2004).

Leaders create an environment that fosters innovation among their followers (Carpenter 2012; Strubler and Redekop 2010). Challenging the status quo is essential to their success (Renko et al. 2015), and they do not take everything at face value. Their ideas could sometimes be radical and deviate from the established norm in the industry (D'Intino et al. 2008). Leaders should be able to make their followers think about old problems in new ways and re-examine assumptions about their roles (Renko et al. 2015).

Problem-Solving Skills

Effective leaders are able to solve problems. They do this by adopting analytical and logical approaches, despite their limited resources. They persist until they find a solution to the problem. This problem-solving orientated mindset concurs with prior research in mainstream leadership literature, with many scholars agreeing that problem-solving skills is an important skill in leadership (Connelly et al. 2000; Mumford et al. 2000a–d; Mumford et al. 2007; Yammarino 2000; Zaccaro et al. 2000) and has an important influence on a leader's performance (Mumford et al. 2000b). It is widely mentioned in entrepreneurial leadership literature that entrepreneurial leaders are able to solve complex business, social and economic problems (Greenberg et al. 2013) and are constantly looking for new problems to solve (Darling et al. 2007).

Envisioning Skills

Envisioning is a core conceptual skill that leaders should possess. Vision involves '...creating a picture of what the future state will be like' (Flamholtz 2011, p. 7). In other words, leaders need to be able to create a vivid picture of the future for the organisation to create added value. When the vision is known and shared, it generates enthusiasm and motivation, and builds the confidence of people in the organisation (Harrison et al. 2016; Karanian 2007; Roomi and Harrison 2011). As stated by Darling et al. (2007, p. 10), 'Vision grabs attention'. Therefore, leaders should be able to communicate the vision to their employees in an exciting and inspirational fashion to ensure implementation (Cogliser and Brigham 2004).

Envisioning the future is fundamental to leadership (Flamholtz 2011; Harrison et al. 2016). According to Paul and Whittam (2015) on leadership development, envisioning works best when a leader views it as a two-stage process. The first stage of envisioning is a reflective activity, whereby a leader envisages an idea. To advance an idea, a leader must cultivate not only a personal vision of how the idea may be achieved but also a deep conviction that it will be successful.

The second stage of the envisioning process requires the individual to sell this vision to a range of diverse stakeholders (Harrison et al. 2016; Paul and Whittam 2015). These can include family, investors and staff members, which altogether comprise the financial muscle and the talent necessary for a start-up to succeed. The requirement places a great demand upon an individual to articulate the future so that these various groups are satisfied.

This two-stage envisioning process can readily be applied by all leaders and not only business or entrepreneurial leaders in other industries. Indeed, the skill of putting envisioning into practice will be easier when leaders follow a two-stage process.

Strategic Planning Skills

Strategic planning skills form another important conceptual skill for any leader, which is paramount to their success. This is not clearly stated in the Katz framework. However, more studies in mainstream leadership literature have identified strategic skills as a core skill for leadership (Mumford et al. 2007; Siewiorek et al. 2012).

Leaders ought to develop strategies for their organisations. They are usually strategically oriented and can formulate strategy based on available resources (Carpenter 2012). They think strategically (Ballein 1998), take a holistic view (Hejazi et al. 2012) and '...develop risk taking and innovative strategies to meet the challenges of the environment, system, community and stakeholders' (Guo 2009, p. 25).

Effective leaders should be able to draft out plans and anticipate changes. While planning, they should be able to forecast and manage their time effectively. It is important that all leaders are involved in strategic planning (Marshall-Mies et al. 2000; Yukl 2010), and that planning in complex and dynamic environments improves performance (Mumford et al. 2002).

Decision-making Skills

Decision-making is a conceptual skill that leaders possess. Leaders are decisive (Ballein 1998; Carpenter 2012; Gupta et al. 2004; Hentschke

2010). These individuals make '...decisions quickly alone or with modest amounts of advice' (Hentschke 2010, p. 122). They are constantly involved in courageous decision-making (D'Intino et al. 2008). However, it is arguable that not all leaders are quick in their decision-making. Rather, it is the quality of the decisions that matter and not the pace.

This section confirms the work of Katz (1974). However, the elements that constitute conceptual skills appear to be more elaborate compared to the findings of Katz. The ability to analyse complex situations, generate new ideas, envision the future, plan strategically, solve problems and make the right decisions are key conceptual skills of an effective leader.

Interpersonal Skills

Based on cumulative studies, interpersonal skills comprise six sub-skills: empathy, communication and listening skills, motivating skills, team-building skills, people management and development, and self-management. These are discussed below.

Empathy

Empathy is a core interpersonal skill that effective leaders possess. Effective leaders understand the feelings, motives and emotions of others. They are empathetic towards their followers. These views confirm the claim found in mainstream leadership literature that leaders should have the ability to understand another person's motives, values and emotions (Yukl 2010). They should be sensitive to the emotions of others (Lord and Hall 2005), since this is a strong predictor of leadership (Kellett et al. 2002). This is also in line with the findings from entrepreneurial leadership literature. Scholars have stated that entrepreneurial leaders should be able to recognise others' emotions (Hejazi et al. 2012), be thoughtful about their associates (Siddiqui 2007) and caring towards their followers (Tarabishy et al. 2002). However, it is arguable that sometimes showing empathy in the form of compassion could be detrimental to profitability for business leaders. Though compassion is necessary, there is a need to strike a balance especially in a turbulent business environment where profit margins are tight. Nevertheless, effective leaders are usually aware of this.

Communication/Listening Skills

Communication and listening skills are necessary for building interpersonal relationships. These help to inspire an understanding of the actions of employees, customers and vendors (Hentschke 2010). It is the '...process of making sense to the world and sharing that sense with others by co-creating meaning through the use of verbal and non-verbal symbols' (Darling and Beebe 2007, p. 152). Leaders must have the ability to listen to all stakeholders in the organisation. By listening to their followers, they are able to make better decisions. This is consistent with the findings of Graham (1983) and Mumford et al. (2007) that leaders must listen actively. For Hentschke (2010, p. 120), '...it is more likely to mean the difference between success and failure'.

Motivating Skills

The ability to motivate and inspire confidence in followers is a vital interpersonal skill for effective leadership. These perceptions concur with prior research in mainstream leadership literature that interpersonal skills are essential for influencing people (Yukl 2010), especially in charismatic, transformational and entrepreneurial leadership (Bass and Avolio 1990; Fernald et al. 2005; Kansikas et al. 2012). Leaders are good motivators and that ability to motivate and communicate is vital (Hentschke 2010). These views resonate with those found in entrepreneurial leadership literature that entrepreneurial leaders are able to communicate in an inspirational fashion to their followers (Cogliser and Brigham 2004). Entrepreneurial leaders inspire the confidence, emotions, beliefs, values and behaviours of others (Gupta et al. 2004; Hejazi et al. 2012). These individuals inspire and influence a group of individuals towards the fulfilment of their goals (Darling et al. 2007).

However, effective leaders are not only proficient in motivating their followers but also should have the ability to motivate themselves.

Team-building Skills

The ability to build teams and promote team work is a vital interpersonal skill for effective leadership. Leaders promote team work (Bagheri and Pihie 2011) and foster team spirit (Strubler and Redekop 2010). They are able to move from 'me to we' (Swiercz and Lydon 2002, p. 387) and induce group members to work together (Gupta et al. 2004). Indeed, leaders are team players (Ballein 1998) and develop effective venture teams (Carpenter 2012; Kuratko and Hornsby 1999).

People Management and Development Skills

The ability to manage and develop people forms an important interpersonal skill in effective leadership. Leaders especially business related need to understand the training needs of their followers (Hejazi et al. 2012) if they are to build high-performance teams in the organisation (Guo 2009). Role modelling is also an important factor in managing people. To demand respect and trust from your followers, it is important to lead by example. Followers learn a lot by looking at their leaders. These perceptions concur with previous research findings that leaders serve as an '…example of opportunity focused behaviour for the followers, creating a culture for innovation' (Renko et al. 2012, p. 180).

Self-Management Skills

The ability of leaders to manage themselves is an essential interpersonal skill. This is evidenced in their planning and organising, in their handling of difficult situations and in their critical reflection on their strengths and weaknesses. Effective leaders have the ability to handle pressure and exhibit self-control in difficult situations, and this is pivotal to their success. They are not flustered and are able to control their emotions. These perceptions are consistent with those found in the literature in the domain of leadership. They are in line with findings in the literature on self-regulation in leaders '…as an ability to channel emotions behaviour that is appropriate for the situation' (Yukl 2010, p. 66). Effective leaders are able to adjust their behaviour according to the situation, which Lord and Hall (2005) refer to as meta-monitoring, and handle stress effectively which makes them more successful.

Effective leaders show a conscious effort to improve their conduct through formal training, or informally by their own reading. Leaders are improvement-oriented (Gupta et al. 2004). According to Day (2001, p. 605), 'Effective leadership occurs through the development of individual leaders'. Leaders may acquire requisite leadership skills through leadership training courses (Mumford et al. 2000a) and human resource (HR) processes (Day et al. 2014).

Good leaders are self-aware, a behaviour '…which is an understanding of one's own moods and emotions' (Yukl 2010, p. 66). These include emotional self-awareness, accurate self-assessment and conscientiousness (Boyatzis et al. 2000). They have an awareness of their cognitive processes (Marshall-Mies et al. 2000). Leaders understand their own strengths and weakness, and get people to complement their weaknesses.

Entrepreneurial Skills

Though this skill is specifically in entrepreneurial leadership literature, it is important for effective leadership; hence, will be addressed in this section. This skill set consists of three skills, namely, opportunity identification, opportunity exploitation and risk management. These are discussed below.

Opportunity Identification Skills

The ability to identify opportunities is an important skill required for successful leadership. It is arguably this skill that distinguishes entrepreneurial leadership from the other types of leadership highlighted in the broader leadership literature. This view is in line with numerous studies on entrepreneurial leadership (e.g. Carpenter 2012; Currie et al. 2008; Gupta et al. 2004; Harrison et al. 2016; Renko et al. 2012; Renko et al. 2015, etc.). Entrepreneurial leaders are apt at recognising opportunities. This reflects the view of Renko et al. (2012) that entrepreneurial leadership is based on the continuous recognition of new opportunities. Entrepreneurial leaders are 'aggressive catalysts' and recognise opportunities, whereas others see 'chaos, contradictions or confusion' (Kuratko 2007, p. 6). Entrepreneurial leaders are good pattern recognisers, seeing roles others do not see (Carpenter 2012). Where other people see problems, entrepreneurial leaders see opportunities (Hentschke 2010). Entrepreneurial leaders recognise new entrepreneurial opportunities and pursue their visions through creative, innovative, even risky tactics (Renko et al. 2012). They constantly seek opportunities for growth (Carpenter 2012).

Opportunity Exploitation Skills

Effective leaders are able to exploit recognised opportunities. Such opportunities may vary from expansion into emerging markets, to selling products with a short shelf life to maximise profitability, etc. This resonates with the common perception found in the literature that entrepreneurial leaders are able to exploit opportunities (Harrison et al. 2016). According to Darling et al. (2007), success for an entrepreneurial leader is not based on intellect; rather, it is attributed to their ability to recognise and exploit opportunities. However, the opportunities may not always be new, but their ability to quickly exploit them is more important.

Risk Management Skills

The risk management element is not reflected within the Katz conceptual framework on leadership. This is not surprising, as risk-taking behaviour is a concept that is more established in entrepreneurship rather than leadership theory. However, this view resonate with research evidence from literature on risk-taking as a characteristic of an entre-preneurial leader (Ahmed and Ramzan 2013; Ballein 1998; Carpenter 2012; Chen 2007; Currie et al. 2008; D'Intino et al. 2008; Gupta et al. 2004; Harrison et al. 2016; Kansikas et al. 2012; Lippitt 1987; Okudan and Rzasa 2006; Renko et al. 2015; Tarabishy et al. 2005). Leaders especially business related should have the ability to manage risks they encounter in their business. They should be able to identify, evaluate and assess risks. Leaders should ruminate on ways to mitigate risks and estimate their impact on the financial position of their companies. Indeed, Guo (2009) highlights risk management as a core competence of an entrepreneurial leader.

Leadership Skills Development

With the emphasis on leadership skills in today's world, it has become paramount that all individuals who aspire to be leaders must know how to develop the required skill set. Some of these methods are discussed below.

Mentoring

Several studies have provided evidence that mentoring is important in leadership development and are helpful in sophisticated mental representations of strategic issues (Day, 2001; Scandura and Schriesheim 1994). Mentoring could be formal or informal. Formal mentoring is a structured programme where a more experienced manager is put in place to support and develop a less experienced individual. The programme could be very beneficial if properly structured. It can improve learning, facilitate adjustment and most importantly develop the leadership skills in the mentee that the mentor may already possess. The mentor serves as a role model. They become exemplars of the behaviour and culture of the organisation from the lens of the mentee. The protégé learns by looking at them.

However, despite the benefits of formal mentoring, it may not always be successful. One of the drawbacks of the process is identifying the right mentor and ensuring that there is a fit between the mentor and the mentee. Most times, this is usually difficult to ascertain due to a variety of factors such as personality, behaviour, age, gender and race (Thomas 1990; Yukl 2010). Studies have provided evidence of the usefulness of informal mentoring (Noe et al. 2002). This type of mentoring does not have the formal programme or schedule. In this case, the protégé is more proactive in building the mentoring relationship.

It is worth stating that though mentoring is a good way of leadership skill development and many scholars agree on its efficacy (Day 2001; Tonidandel et al. 2007), there are still some contrary views (Cox and Jennings 1995). Not all successful leaders have been identified to have mentors. Some of these leaders developed their skills through facing adversity. In summary, many self-made business leaders may not see themselves as having a specific mentor.

Leadership Training Programmes

Leadership training programmes are widely used to develop leadership skills in organisations. Almost every organisation whether small or large has a leadership programme in place to develop their staff. These programmes may take different forms ranging from short leadership workshops in few hours/days to structured university programmes in form of MBAs or DBAs. Many of the organisations even go to the extent of hiring consultants to design leadership training programmes that meet the specific needs of the establishment. They consider it important to develop staff through training and other activities regardless of its cost implication. Though some of these programmes might be expensive in the short term, there is always a cost saving benefit in the long term if it is properly conducted.

Studies have shown that well-timed training interventions can promote the development of leadership skills (Bass 1990; Day 2001; Mumford et al. 2000a; Paul and Whittam 2015). However, similar to mentoring, the efficacy of leadership training programmes is based on its design. The content must be meaningful and the objectives clear (Yukl 2010). The training programme should be tailored to meet the leadership development needs of the organisation. If all these are not incorporated into the programme, it risks becoming an expensive venture that does not add value to both the individual and the organisation.

Personal Growth Activities

Despite the consensus view that mentoring and leadership training programmes are useful in developing leadership competencies, these two techniques emphasise on what organisations actually do to develop the leadership skills of their work force. Leadership development is also a personal journey, and individuals need to commit to developing their own skills.

There are several techniques through which individuals can develop their leadership skills personally. Personal growth activities include reading leadership development books as well as listening and watching programmes on leadership. Individuals need to be aware of their strengths and weaknesses. As regards their weaknesses, personal growth activities should be in place to address them. This can only be possible through emotional self-awareness, accurate self-assessment and conscientiousness (Boyatzis et al. 2000). Indeed, effective leadership requires a high level of emotional development. Only through understanding yourself in form of your feelings and cognitive processes, you will be able to develop the leadership competences required for success in the twenty-first century.

Summary

In this chapter, the skills required for effective leadership were discussed. These skills can be developed through mentoring, leadership training programmes and personal growth activities. Prospective leaders should be trained to develop such skills, and existing leaders should be trained to understand how to balance such competencies, as well as to reflect on their limitations. All organisations can develop and expand the skills of their leaders, thereby increasing the chance for success.

References

Agbim, K. C., Oriarewo, G. O., & Owutuamor, Z. B. (2013). An exploratory study of the entrepreneurial leadership capabilities of entrepreneurs in Anambra state, Nigeria. *Journal of Business Management & Social Sciences Research, 2*(9), 68–75.

Ahmed, A., & Ramzan, M. (2013). A learning and improvement model in entrepreneurial leadership. *IOSR Journal of Business and Management, 11*(6), 50–60.

Bagheri, A., & Pihie, Z. A. L. (2011). On becoming an entrepreneurial leader: A focus on the impacts of university entrepreneurship programs. *American Journal of Applied Sciences, 8*(9), 884–892.

Ballein, K. M. (1998). Entrepreneurial leadership characteristics of SNEs emerge as their role develops. *Nursing Administration Quarterly, 22*(2), 60–69.

Bass, B. M. (1990). *Bass and Stogdills handbook of leadership*. New York: Free Press.

Bass, B. M., & Avolio, B. J. (1990). *Transformational leadership development: Manual for multifactor leadership questionnaire*. California: Palo Alto Consulting Psychologists Press.

Boyatzis, R. R. (1982). *The competent manager: A model for effective performance*. New York: Wiley.

Boyatzis, R. E., Goleman, D., & Rhee, K. (2000). Clustering competence in emotional intelligence: Insights from the emotional competence inventory (ECI). In R. Bar-On & D. A. J. Parker (Eds.), *Handbook of emotional intelligence* (pp. 343–362). San Francisco, California: Jossey-Bass.

Carpenter, M. T. H. (2012). Cheerleader, opportunity seeker, and master strategist: ARL directors as entrepreneurial leaders. *College & Research Libraries, 73*(1), 11–32.

Chen, M. (2007). Entrepreneurial leadership & new ventures: Creativity in entrepreneurial teams. *Creativity & Innovation Management, 16*(3), 239–249.

Cogliser, C. C., & Brigham, K. H. (2004). The intersection of leadership and entrepreneurship: Mutual lessons to be learned. *The Leadership Quarterly, 15*(6), 771–799.

Connelly, M. S., Gilbert, J. A., Zaccaro, S. J., Threlfall, K., Marks, M. A., & Mumford, M. D. (2000). Exploring the relationship of leadership skills and knowledge to leader performance. *The Leadership Quarterly, 11*(1), 65–86.

Copeman, G. (1971). *The chief executive and business growth*. London: Leviathan House.

Cox, C., & Jennings, R. (1995). The foundations of success: The development and characteristics of British entrepreneurs and intrapreneurs. *Leadership & Organization Development Journal, 16*(7), 4–9.

Currie, G., Humphreys, M., Ucbasaran, D., & Mcmanus, S. (2008). Entrepreneurial leadership in the English public sector: Paradox or possibility? *Public Administration, 86*(4), 987–1008.

Darling, J. R., & Beebe, S. A. (2007). Enhancing entrepreneurial leadership: A focus on key communication priorities. *Journal of Small Business & Entrepreneurship, 20*(2), 151–167.

Darling, J. R., Gabrielsson, M., & Seristö, H. (2007). Enhancing contemporary entrepreneurship: A focus on management leadership. *European Business Review, 19*(1), 4–22.

Day, D. V. (2001). Leadership development: A review in context. *The Leadership Quarterly, 11*(4), 581–613.

Day, D. V., Fleenor, J. W., Atwater, L. E., Sturm, R. E., & McKee, R. A. (2014). Advances in leader and leadership development: A review of 25 years of research and theory. *The Leadership Quarterly, 25*(1), 63–82.

D'Intino, R. S., Boyles, T., Neck, C. P., & Hall, J. R. (2008). Visionary entrepreneurial leadership in the aircraft industry: The Boeing company legacy. *Journal of Management History, 14*(1), 39–54.

Fernald, L. W., Jr., Solomon, G. T., & Tarabishy, A. (2005). A new paradigm: Entrepreneurial leadership. *Southern Business Review, 30*(2), 1–10.

Flamholtz, E. G. (2011). The leadership molecule hypothesis: Implications for entrepreneurial organizations. *International Review of Entrepreneurship, 9*(3), 1–23.

Gillen, D. J., & Carroll, S. J., Jr. (1985). Relationship of managerial ability to unit effectiveness in more organic versus more mechanistic departments. *Journal of Management Studies, 22*(6), 61–75.

Gordon, A., & Yukl, G. (2004). The future of leadership research: Challenges and opportunities. *German Journal of Research in Human Resource Management, 8*(3), 359–365.

Graham, J. L. (1983). Brazilian, Japanese, and American business negotiations. *Journal of International Business Studies, 14*(1), 47–61.

Greenberg, D., McKone-Sweet, K., & Wilson, H. J. (2013). Entrepreneurial leaders: Creating opportunity in an unknowable world. *Leader to Leader, 2013*(67), 56–62.

Guo, K. L. (2009). Core competencies of the entrepreneurial leader in health care organizations. *Health Care Manager, 28*(1), 19–29.

Gupta, V., Macmillan, I. C., & Surie, G. (2004). Entrepreneurial leadership: Developing and measuring a cross-cultural construct. *Journal of Business Venturing, 19*(2), 241–260.

Haq, S. (2011). Ethics and leadership skills in the public service. *Procedia-Social and Behavioral Sciences, 15*(2011), 2792–2796.

Harris, K. J., Kacmar, K. M., Zivnuska, S., & Shaw, J. D. (2007). The impact of political skill on impression management effectiveness. *Journal of Applied Psychology, 92*(1), 278–285.

Harrison, C., Paul, S., & Burnard, K. (2016). Entrepreneurial leadership in retail pharmacy: Developing economy perspective. *Journal of Workplace Learning, 28*(3), 150–167.

Hejazi, A. M., Maleki, M. M., & Naeji, M. J. (2012). Designing a scale for measuring entrepreneurial leadership in SME's. *International Proceedings of Economics Development and Research, 28*(1), 71–77.

Hentschke, G. C. (2010). Developing entrepreneurial leaders. In B. Davies & M. Brundrett (Eds.), *Developing successful leadership* (pp. 115–132). Netherlands: Springer.

Jacobs, T. O., & Jaques, E. (1987). Leadership in complex systems. In J. A. Zeidner (Ed.), *Human productivity enhancement, Vol. II: Organizations, personnel, and decision making* (pp. 201–245). New York: Praeger.

Kansikas, J., Laakkonen, A., Sarpo, V., & Kontinen, T. (2012). Entrepreneurial leadership and familiness as resources for strategic entrepreneurship. *International Journal of Entrepreneurial Behaviour & Research, 18*(2), 141–158.

Karanian, B. (2007). Entrepreneurial leadership: A balancing act in engineering and science. *American Society for Engineering Education (ASEE), AC 2007-2804: Entrepreneurial Leadership and Transformational Change Global Colloquia*, Rio de Janeiro, Brazil.

Katz, R. L. (1955). Skills of an effective administrator. *Harvard Business Review, 33*(1), 33–42.

Katz, R. L. (1974). Skills of an effective administrator. *Harvard Business Review, 52*(5), 90–102.

Kellett, J. B., Humphrey, R. H., & Sleeth, R. G. (2002). Empathy and complex task performance: Two routes to leadership. *The Leadership Quarterly, 13*(5), 523–544.

Kuratko, D. F. (2007). Entrepreneurial leadership in the 21st century. *Journal of Leadership & Organizational Studies, 13*(4), 1–11.

Kuratko, D. F., & Hornsby, J. S. (1999). Corporate entrepreneurial leadership for the 21st century. *Journal of Leadership & Organizational Studies, 5*(2), 27–39.

Lippitt, G. L. (1987). Entrepreneurial leadership: A performing art. *The Journal of Creative Behavior, 21*(3), 264–270.

Lord, R. G., & Hall, R. J. (2005). Identity, deep structure and the development of leadership skill. *The Leadership Quarterly, 16*(4), 591–615.

Luthans, F., Welsh, D. H., & Taylor, L. A. (1988). A descriptive model of managerial effectiveness. *Group & Organization Studies, 13*(2), 148–162.

Mahoney, T. A., Jerdee, T. H., & Carroll, S. J., Jr. (1963). *Development of managerial performance: A research approach.* Cincinnati: South-Western.

Mahoney, T. A., Jerdee, T. H., & Carroll, S. J., Jr. (1965). The jobs of management. *Industrial Relations, 4*(2), 97–110.

Marshall-Mies, J. C., Fleishman, E. A., Martin, J. A., Zaccaro, S. J., Baughman, W. A., & McGee, M. L. (2000). Development and evaluation of cognitive and metacognitive measures for predicting leadership potential. *The Leadership Quarterly, 11*(1), 135–153.

McCall, M. W., & Lombardo, M. M. (1983). *Off the track: Why and how successful managers get derailed* (Tech. Rep. No 21). Greensboro, North Carolina: Center for Creative Leadership.

Mintzberg, H. (1973). *The nature of managerial work.* New York: Harper and Row.

Mumford, M. D., Zaccaro, S. J., Harding, F. D., Jacobs, T. O., & Fleishman, E. A. (2000a). Leadership skills for a changing world solving complex social problems. *The Leadership Quarterly, 11*(1), 11–35.

Mumford, M. D., Marks, M. A., Connelly, M. S., Zaccaro, S. J., & Reiter-Palmon, R. (2000b). Development of leadership skills: Experience and timing. *The Leadership Quarterly, 11*(1), 87–114.

Mumford, M. D., Zaccaro, S. J., Johnson, J. F., Diana, M., Gilbert, J. A., & Threlfall, K. (2000c). Patterns of leader characteristics: Implications for performance and development. *The Leadership Quarterly, 11*(1), 115–133.

Mumford, M. D., Zaccaro, S. J., Connelly, M. S., & Marks, M. A. (2000d). Leadership skills: Conclusions and future directions. *The Leadership Quarterly, 11*(1), 155–170.

Mumford, M. D., Scott, G. M., Gaddis, B., & Strange, J. M. (2002). Leading creative people: Orchestrating expertise and relationships. *The Leadership Quarterly, 13*(6), 705–750.

Mumford, T. V., Campion, M. A., & Morgeson, F. P. (2007). The leadership skills strataplex: Leadership skill requirements across organizational levels. *The Leadership Quarterly, 18*(2), 154–166.

Noe, R. A., Greenberger, D. B., & Wang, S. (2002). Mentoring: What we know and where we might go. In G. R. Ferris & J. J. Martocchio (Eds.), *Research in personnel and human resources management* (pp. 129–173). Oxford: Emerald Group Publishing Limited.

Northouse, P. G. (2010). *Leadership: Theory and practice* (5th ed.). California: Sage.

Okudan, G. E., & Rzasa, S. E. (2006). A project-based approach to entrepreneurial leadership education. *Technovation, 26*(2), 195–210.

Paul, S., & Whittam, G. (2015). The show must go on: Leadership learning on Broadway. *Organizational Dynamics, 44*(3), 196–203.

Pavett, C. M., & Lau, A. W. (1983). Managerial work: The influence of hierarchical level and functional specialty. *Academy of Management Journal, 26*(1), 170–177.

Renko, M., Tarabishy, A., Carsrud, A. L., & Brännback, M. (2012). Entrepreneurial leadership and the family business. In A. L. Carsrud & M. Brännback (Eds.), *Understanding family businesses: Undiscovered approaches, unique perspectives and neglected topics* (pp. 169–184). New York: Springer.

Renko, M., Tarabishy, A., Carsrud, A. L., & Brannback, M. (2015). Understanding & measuring entrepreneurial leadership. *Journal of Small Business Management, 53*(1), 54–74.

Roomi, M. A., & Harrison, P. (2011). Entrepreneurial leadership: What is it & how should it be taught? *International Review of Entrepreneurship, 9*(3), 1–44.

Scandura, T. A., & Schriesheim, C. A. (1994). Leader-member exchange and supervisor career mentoring as complementary constructs in leadership research. *Academy of Management Journal, 37*(6), 1588–1602.

Schedlitzki, D., & Edwards, G. (2014). *Studying leadership: Traditional and critical approaches*. London: Sage.

Shiba, S. (1998). Leadership and breakthrough. *Centre for Quality Management Journal, 7*(2), 10–22.

Shipper, F., & Dillard, J. E., Jr. (2000). A study of impending derailment and recovery of middle managers across career stages. *Human Resource Management, 39*(4), 331–345.

Siddiqui, S. (2007). An empirical study of traits determining entrepreneurial leadership-An educational perspective. *Skyline Business Review, 4*(1), 37–44.

Siewiorek, A., Saarinen, E., Lainema, T., & Lehtinen, E. (2012). Learning leadership skills in a simulated business environment. *Computers & Education, 58*(1), 121–135.

Strubler, D. C., & Redekop, B. W. (2010). Entrepreneurial human resource leadership: A conversation with Dwight Carlson. *Human Resource Management, 49*(4), 793–804.

Swiercz, P. M., & Lydon, S. R. (2002). Entrepreneurial leadership in high-tech firms: A field study. *Leadership & Organization Development Journal, 23*(7), 380–389.

Tarabishy, A., Fernald Jr, L. W., & Solomon, G. T. (2002). *Understanding entrepreneurial leadership in today's dynamic markets.* Washington: School of Business and Public Management, Department of Management Science, The George Washington University Publication.

Tarabishy, A., Solomon, G., Fernald, L. W., Jr., & Sashkin, M. (2005). The entrepreneurial leader's impact on the organization's performance in dynamic markets. *The Journal of Private Equity, 8*(4), 20–29.

Thomas, D. A. (1990). The impact of race on managers' experiences of developmental relationships (mentoring and sponsorship): An intra-organizational study. *Journal of Organizational Behavior, 11*(6), 479–492.

Tonidandel, S., Avery, D. R., & Phillips, M. G. (2007). Maximizing returns on mentoring: Factors affecting subsequent protégé performance. *Journal of Organizational Behavior, 28*(1), 89–110.

Westley, F., & Mintzberg, H. (1989). Visionary leadership and strategic management. *Strategic Management Journal, 10*(S1), 17–32.

Wright, P. (1996). *Managerial leadership.* London: Routledge.

Wright, P. L., & Taylor, D. S. (1994). *Improving leadership performance: Skills for effective leadership* (2nd ed.). Hemel Hempstead, Herts: Prentice-Hall.

Yammarino, F. J. (2000). Leadership skills: Introduction and overview. *The Leadership Quarterly, 11*(1), 5–9.

Yukl, G. (1989). Managerial leadership: A review of theory and research. *Journal of Management, 15*(2), 251–289.

Yukl, G. (2010). *Leadership in organisations* (7th ed.) Upper Saddle River, New Jersey: Pearson Education Limited.

Zaccaro, S. J., & Klimoski, R. J. (2001). The nature of organizational leadership: An introduction. In S. J. Zaccaro & R. J. Klimoski (Eds.), *The nature of organizational leadership: Understanding the performance imperatives confronting today's leaders* (pp. 3–41). San Francisco, California: Jossey-Bass.

Zaccaro, S. J., Mumford, M. D., Connelly, M. S., Marks, M. A., & Gilbert, J. A. (2000). Assessment of leader problem-solving capabilities. *The Leadership Quarterly, 11*(1), 37–64.

Index

A

Abraham, Laura 45
Achievement Orientation 20, 59
Activities
    authentic leadership 16, 34,
        53–55, 62, 65
    charismatic leadership 16, 20, 34,
        41–44, 47, 65
    contingency perspective 16,
        26–29
    distributed leadership 16, 34, 51,
        52, 65
    entrepreneurial leadership 16, 20,
        21, 34, 40, 45, 49, 57–63,
        65
    Great Man theory 16–19, 21, 29
    implicit leadership theory 16, 34,
        35, 65
    leader-member exchange 16,
        34–37, 65
    leadership style 23–25, 27, 28,
        44, 60
    leadership traits 16, 19, 20, 23,
        25, 34, 35, 41, 42, 51, 84
    Manager or Leader? 9
    servant leadership 16, 34, 37–41,
        65
    skill perspective- Apollo 13 21
    transactional leadership 16, 34,
        36, 45–48, 65
    transformational leadership 16,
        20, 34, 39, 47–49, 54, 62,
        65, 89
Amazon 9, 10
Analytical skills 85
Apollo 13 21, 22
Apple 49, 50
Authentic leadership
    activity of 53, 55
    authenticity 55

empirical evidence, lack of 54, 55
ethics 54
integrity 54
moral dimension 54
self-awareness 54
self-knowledge 54
trust 54
values 54
Authority 3, 18, 24
Autocratic leadership style 23

B
Barclays 55–57
Behaviour 3–5, 16, 24, 25, 29, 34,
    35, 42, 47, 51, 56, 57, 62,
    81, 82, 90–94
Behavioural theory
    activity of 23–25, 29
    consideration behaviours 24
    empirical evidence, lack of 27
    employee orientation 24
    initiating structure behaviours 24
    leadership grid 24, 25
    production orientation 24
Bezos, Jeff 9
Blake and Mouton managerial grid
    24
Brown, George 36
Business skill
    leadership development 84

C
Change 6–8, 18, 29, 37, 40, 43, 47,
    49, 60, 64, 65
Charisma 41–43
Charismatic leadership theory
    activity of 42, 43
    empirical evidence, lack of 43

Cognitive skill 85
Communication and listening skills
    88, 89
Compassion 88, 89
Competencies 21, 61, 63, 80, 95
Conceptual skill
    analytical skills 85
    decision making skills 87
    envisioning skills 86
    idea generation skills 85
    problem solving skills 86
    strategic planning skills 87
    strategic skills 83, 87
Consideration behaviours 24
Contingency theory
    activity of 27–29
    empirical evidence, lack of 29
    Fiedler's contingency model 27, 28
    leader–member relations 28
    Least preferred co-worker (LPC)
        scale 28
    position power 28
    relationship-oriented 28
    situational favourableness 28
    task-oriented 28
    task structure 28
Contingent reward 45, 46, 49
Controlling 3, 7, 10
Creativity 48, 59, 83
Culture 10, 46, 52, 60, 63, 90, 93

D
Decision-making
    roles 7
    skill 87
Democratic leadership style 23
Determination 18, 19, 49, 61
Diamond, Bob 55–57

Distributed leadership
    activity of 51, 52
    democratic leadership 51
    empirical evidence, lack of 52
    participative leadership 51
    shared leadership 51
    team leadership 51
Dominance 20

E
Emerging Paradigms 29
Emotional self-awareness 91, 95
Empathy 8, 38, 82, 88
Employee orientation 24
Entrepreneur 7, 9, 60, 61, 81
Entrepreneurial leaders
    attributes of 59, 60
    characteristics of 59
    entrepreneurial skills
        opportunity exploitation skills
            92; opportunity identifica-
            tion skills 91; risk manage-
            ment skills 58, 91, 92
    skills of 91
Entrepreneurial leadership
    compared with other forms of
        leadership 58, 62
    conceptions of 58
    context 58, 60, 61, 63
    a convergence of entrepreneurship
        and leadership 58
    definition of 57
    education 58, 62, 63
    psychological and behavioural pro-
        file of entrepreneurial leaders
        58, 59
    theoretical approach 61
    and values 58, 62

    and venture performance 58, 63
Entrepreneurial skills
    opportunity exploitation skills 92
    opportunity identification skills 91
    risk management skills 92
Envisioning 25, 86, 87
Envisioning skills 86
Ethics
    definition of leadership 6, 62
    entrepreneurial leadership 62
    transformational leadership 54

F
Followers
    attributions about leaders 34
    authentic leadership 53–55
    charismatic leadership 41–43
    conceptual skills 86
    definitions of leadership 6, 34
    distributed leadership 51
    entrepreneurial leadership 57, 88,
        89
    interpersonal skills 89
    leader–member exchange 35, 36
    servant leadership 37, 38, 40
    transactional leadership 45
    transformational leadership 47, 48

G
Great Man theory
    activity of 16, 19
    empirical evidence, lack of 27, 52
    gender 18
Group
    definitions of leadership 4–6, 35,
        37
    distributed leadership 51
    leader–member exchange 37

H

Harry, Charles 40, 41
Human skill 82

I

Idea generation skills 85
Idealised influence 47
Implicit leadership theories
    activity of 16, 34, 35, 65
    attribution 34
    empirical evidence, lack of 16
    perception 35
Individualised consideration 47, 48
Influence
    charismatic leadership 42, 43
    conceptual skills 83
    definitions of leadership 3, 6, 40
    distributed leadership 51
    entrepreneurial leadership 58, 59,
        86
    human skills 81, 82
    interpersonal skills 82
    leadership and management 3, 10
    servant leadership 39
    transactional leadership 45
    transformational leadership 47
Information processing roles 7
In-group members 36
Initiating structure behaviours 24
Initiative 19
Innovation 22, 50, 58–61, 64, 85, 90
Inspirational motivation 47
Integrity 20, 39, 54, 84
Intellectual stimulation 47, 48
Intelligence 19, 20, 84
Interpersonal roles 7
Interpersonal skills

communication and listening skills
    88
empathy 88
motivating skills 88
people management and develop-
    ment 88
self-management 88
team building skills 88
Iowa State University studies 23

J

Jobs, Steve 49, 50

K

Knowledge 2, 21, 25, 28, 51, 80, 81
Kranz, Gene 22, 23

L

Laissez-faire leadership style 23
Leader-member exchange (LMX)
        theory
    activity of 16, 34–37, 65
    empirical evidence, lack of 36
Leaders
    roles of 92
Leadership
    ability 3, 6, 34, 42, 53, 58, 59, 83,
        85, 88–91, 93
    and management 2, 3, 45, 46, 82
    approaches 16, 29, 34, 47, 58, 60,
        62, 65, 83, 86
    behaviour 5, 16, 18, 23–25, 29,
        34, 35, 41, 42, 48
    definitions of 2, 4, 57
    process of influence 3, 6, 39, 42,
        43, 59

research 2, 16, 19, 25, 60
theory
  authentic leadership 53, 55,
    62; charismatic leadership
    41, 43, 44, 47; contingency
    16, 26–29, 34; distributed
    leadership 51, 52; entrepre-
    neurial leadership 16, 34,
    57–63, 65, 84, 85, 91; Great
    Man 16–19, 21, 29; implicit
    leadership 16, 34, 35, 65;
    leader–member exchange
    16, 34, 65; servant leader-
    ship 37–41; skill 34, 83, 95;
    strengths and weaknesses
    65, 66, 83, 90, 95; trait 16,
    19–21, 23, 25, 29, 34, 43,
    60; transactional leadership
    45–49; transformational
    leadership 20, 39, 47–49, 62
  timeline 16
Leadership grid 24
Leadership skills
  business 84
  conceptual 80, 83
  entrepreneurial 21
  human 91
  interpersonal 80
  technical 80, 81
Leadership skills development
  leadership training programmes
    94, 95
  mentoring 93–95
  personal growth activities 95
Leadership style 23, 26–28, 44
Leadership training programmes 80,
    94, 95

Least preferred co-worker (LPC) scale
    28
Literature review 2, 61, 65
London inter-bank offered rate
    (LIBOR) 55, 56

M

Management
  and leadership 2, 7, 8
  definition of 54
  functions of 3, 7
Management-by-exception 45, 46
Managerial grid 24
Managerial roles 7
Managers 2, 3, 7–9, 11, 18, 23, 26,
    36, 58
Mentoring
  formal 93, 94
  role model 93
Motivating skills 88, 89
Multifactor leadership questionnaire
    (MLQ) 47, 48

N

Need for affiliation 20
Need for power 20
Negotiation 4, 36, 82

O

Ohio State University studies 23, 24
O' Leary, Michael 26
Opportunity exploitation skills 92
Opportunity identification skills 91
Organisations
  authentic leadership theory 54
  behavioural theory 23

charismatic leadership theory 42
conceptual skills 87
contingency theory 29
entrepreneurial leadership theory 61
human skills 81
interpersonal skills 80, 88–90
leader-member exchange theory 16, 34–36
leadership 2, 8, 23, 24, 29, 39, 41, 42, 47, 52–54, 61, 94, 95
leadership skills development 94, 95
management 8, 54, 81
servant leadership theory 37, 39, 40
technical skills 81
transformational leadership theory 39
Out-group members 36

P

Participative leadership 51
Path goal theory 45
People management and development skills
    role model 90
Persistence 19, 59
Personal growth activities 80, 95
Personality 19–21, 28, 44, 94
Peters, Grace 52
Phenomenon 3, 16, 40, 58, 65
Planning 3, 7, 10, 59, 83, 87, 90
Position power 28
Power 4, 18, 22, 38, 42
Problem-solving skills 86
Process 3–6, 34, 42, 46, 51, 52, 54, 61, 86, 87, 89, 93

Production orientation 24
Purpose 5, 8

R

Relationship-oriented 28
Research 2, 16, 18–21, 25, 27, 28, 35–37, 39, 40, 43, 45, 48, 49, 51, 53, 54, 59, 60, 62, 67, 80, 81, 84, 86, 89, 90, 92
Risk 45, 46, 59, 61, 85, 87, 91–93
Risk management skill 58, 91, 92
Rivler 36, 37
Role model 93
Ryanair 26, 27

S

Self-awareness 54
Self-confidence 19, 20
Self-interest 38
Self-knowledge 54
Self-management skills
    leadership skill development 90
Self-regulation 54, 91
Servant leadership
    activity of 37–39
    attributes of 39, 41
    characteristics of 38
    empirical evidence, lack of 39
Shared leadership 51
Situational favourableness 28
Skill 16, 21, 23, 29, 80, 85–91, 93, 94
Skill theory 21, 80, 82
    activity of 21, 29
    approach 21, 23
    business skills 81, 84

conceptual skills 21
empirical evidence, lack of 25
entrepreneurial skills 21
human skills 81, 82
interpersonal skills 90
perspective 21, 25, 29
technical skills 80, 82, 84
Strategic planning skills 87

T
Task-oriented 25, 28
Team-building skills 88, 90
Team leadership 51
Technical skill 80
Theory 16–20, 23, 25–29, 34–38,
    42–45, 47, 48, 51, 53, 54,
    57, 61, 65, 92
Timeline showing the approaches to
    leadership 17
Trait theory
    activity of 19
    empirical evidence, lack of 16
    leadership traits 16, 20, 25, 35
Transactional leadership
    activity of 16
    contingent reward 45, 46, 49
    empirical evidence, lack of 51

management-by-exception 45
Transformational leadership
    activity of 16
    empirical evidence, lack of 54
    multifactor leadership question-
        naire (MLQ) 47, 48
Trust 8, 24, 36–39, 41, 47, 53, 54,
    60, 90

U
University of Michigan studies 23, 24

V
Values 4, 25, 43, 54, 58, 62, 88, 89
Vertical dyad linkage theory (VDL)
    35
Vision 7, 27, 39, 42, 48, 50, 59, 60,
    64, 65, 86, 87
Visionary leadership 48

W
Women 18

CPI Antony Rowe
Chippenham, UK
2018-10-18 10:41